COLLECTOR'S VALUE GUIDE

D1072718

BOYDS BEARS & FRIENDS

The Bearstone Collection®
The Folkstone Collection®
The Purrstone Collection™
The Dollstone Collection™
The Shoe Box Bears™

Collector Handbook
and Secondary Market Price Guide

FIFTH EDITION

⟨ BOYDS BEARS & FRIENDS ⟩™

"The Bearstone Collection®" and "The Folkstone Collection®" are registered trademarks of The Boyds Collection Ltd. "The Wee Folkstones™," "The Purrstone Collection™," "The Dollstone Collection™," "Yesterday's Child . . .™," "The Shoe Box Bears™," "DeskAnimals™," "Bearly-Built Villages™," "Bearwear™," "Folkwear™," "Le Bearmoge™" and "Bearware Potteryworks™" are trademarks of The Boyds Collection Ltd. The Boyds Collection Ltd. and associated trademarks, copyrights and photography are owned by The Boyds Collection Ltd. and are used under license. All Rights Reserved. The Boyds Collection Ltd. is not affiliated with CheckerBee Publishing nor shares the opinions expressed in this publication.

Managing Editor:	Jeff Mahony	Creative Director:	Joe T. Nguyen
Associate Editors:	Melissa A. Bennett	Production Supervisor:	Scott Sierakowski
	Jan Cronan	Senior Graphic Designers:	Lance Doyle
	Gia C. Manalio		Susannah C. Judd
	Paula Stuckart		David S. Maloney
Contributing Editor:	Mike Micciulla		Carole Mattia-Slater
Editorial Assistants:	Jennifer Filipek	Graphic Designers:	Jennifer J. Bennett
	Nicole LeGard Lenderking		Sean-Ryan Dudley
	Joan C. Wheal		Kimberly Eastman
Research Assistants:	Timothy R. Affleck		Jason C. Jasch
	Priscilla Berthiaume		Angi Shearstone
	Heather N. Carreiro		David Ten Eyck
	Beth Hackett	Web Graphic Designer:	Ryan Falis
	Victoria Puorro		
	Steven Shinkaruk		
Web Reporters:	Samantha Bouffard		
	Ren Messina		

ISBN 1-888-914-76-9

CHECKERBEE™ and COLLECTOR'S VALUE GUIDE™ are trademarks of CheckerBee, Inc.
Copyright© by CheckerBee, Inc. 2000.
All rights reserved. No part of this book may be reproduced or transmitted in any form or by any means, electronic or mechanical, including photocopying, recording, or by any information storage or retrieval system, without the written permission of the publisher.

306 Industrial Park Road • Middletown, CT 06457
www.collectorbee.com

Contents

Contents

Introducing The Collector's Value Guide™

*W*hen Gary M. Lowenthal crafted his first Bearstone pieces in 1993, he couldn't have foreseen that his creations would some day be valued as collectibles. But seven years and five additional collections later, Lowenthal's whimsical carvings have become some of the most sought-after items in the collectibles world – and "The Head Bean" shows no signs of slowing down. The Collector's Value Guide™ is designed to help you keep up with Lowenthal's steady stream of new products and ideas!

This all-new, fifth edition of the Boyds Bears & Friends Collector's Value Guide™ is designed to guide you through the marvelous world of Boyds resin figurines and accessories – both old and new. You'll find the latest information on secondary market values, the next pieces slated to be retired and the newest releases from "Yer Ol' Uncle Bean!" If you just can't get enough of these delightful bears, rabbits, angels and other charming creatures, let this book be your guide to the ever-expanding world of Boyds resin! But that's not all! Inside this book, you'll also find:

- A look at the newest pieces to join the resin family, including The Purrstone Collection™ and Bearly-Built Villages™.

- First-hand accounts from collectors who've met "The Head Bean Hisself" and share what Gary Lowenthal is really like.

- The latest news from The Loyal Order of Friends of Boyds, and a spotlight on the new exclusive club pieces.

- Information about other Boyds collections, including plush animals, Le Bearmoge™ and Bearware Potteryworks™.

- How to best insure your Boyds collection so your family will enjoy your figurines for generations to come.

All About Boyds

*I*t's been more than 20 years since "The Head Bean" opened shop and began delighting collectors throughout the world with his unique creations. But just how did Gary M. Lowenthal, creator and purveyor of all things Boyds, turn a line of wooden duck decoys and "Gnome Homes" into the world-famous Boyds Collection? Well, it all started with a desire to leave city life behind.

Born and raised in Manhattan, Lowenthal returned to New York City after a post-college stint in the Fiji Islands with the Peace Corps. Here he embarked on a seven-year career with Bloomingdales, where he learned the ins and outs of purchasing, design and merchandising. Lowenthal was a man with a dream, however, so he and his then-girlfriend (now wife), Tina, left Bloomingdales and "The Big City" to open an antiques shop in Boyds, Maryland.

The couple soon realized the antiques business wasn't for them. After a few false starts, they began selling a line of hand-carved duck decoys, and, later, a line of ceramic houses called "Gnome Homes." Their product line grew to include plush bears in 1981. Then in 1987, Lowenthal packed up the family and moved again, this time to Gettysburg, Pennsylvania, where he established The Boyds Collection Ltd.

As the plush line grew, so did the company's success. In 1993, The Bearstone Collection®, a line of resin figures based on the plush line, made its debut. The Folkstone Collection® followed in 1994, with Yesterday's Child . . . The Dollstone Collection™ and The Shoe Box Bears™ appearing in 1996, DeskAnimals™ in 1998, The Purrstone Collection in 1999 and the Bearly-Built Villages in 2000. Each collection perfectly embodies the whimsy and wonder that have won "Ol' Uncle Bean" such a loyal following.

THE BEARSTONE COLLECTION – The intricately detailed resin figurines feature familiar friends from the plush line captured in a variety of situations and settings. Most pieces are available in four different editions, each limited to quantities of 6,000 pieces. The *Holiday Pageant Series* and *Noah's Pageant Series*, however, have 7,200 pieces per edition. There are 18 new Bearstone pieces for Spring 2000, as well as one piece in the new *Classic Beary Tales Series*, featuring Bearstones in fairy tale scenes.

THE FOLKSTONE COLLECTION – These "pencil-style" figurines are one of the more unique branches of the Boyds family tree. These lanky animals come in an assortment of personalities and professions, and in editions of 6,000 pieces each. Within the land of Folkstone, there are two series: *Carvers Choice* and *The Wee Folkstones*™.

The *Carvers Choice* resin pieces are reminiscent of the folk art style of Boyds' early days. Larger than their Folkstone pals, the *Carvers Choice* pieces have the look of hand carved wood and feature a sub-series called *Santa & Friends*. There are six new *Carvers Choice* pieces for Spring 2000.

The *Wee Folkstones* series is a group of little folk, including fairies, Not Quite Guardian Angels (or N.Q.G.A.) and snowpeople. The *Wee Folkstones* also include three sub-groups: *Ribbit & Co.*, a collection of frogs in search of a good pond, tasty flies and a kiss or two from a pretty princess;

Penguins, a group of nattily-dressed creatures ready for a formal affair (or some winter fun) who joined the Boyds family in 1999; and *The Garden Gang*, which made its debut in Spring 2000 with two pieces inspired by the country life.

THE PURRSTONE COLLECTION – Cozying into the hearts of cat-loving collectors everywhere, these cuddle-some kitties made their debut in 1999 with six pieces, including a limited edition. Exquisitely crafted, these cats bear two hallmarks: Boyds' famous paw print and a cat nose and whiskers. Six more friendly felines joined the collection for Spring 2000.

YESTERDAY'S CHILD · THE DOLLSTONE COLLECTION – Introduced in 1995 on the home shopping television show QVC, these resin figurines and accessories have captured the hearts of collectors with their depiction of the innocent days of childhood, when teddy bears were our best friends and make-believe was real. Seven pieces were added to the line for 2000, including a waterglobe and a musical.

YESTERDAY'S CHILD . . .™ THE DOLL COLLECTION – Two 16" limited edition porcelain dolls joined the Boyds family in 1997, each with production runs of 9,600 pieces. Since 1998, the new dolls have had production runs of 12,000 pieces each. Designed with resin hands and feet, the hand cast, hand painted and numbered creations now total 42, including 12 open-edition 12" dolls, which were introduced to the line in 1999.

THE SHOE BOX BEARS – As a young boy, Lowenthal kept his small toys and treasures in shoe boxes, thus inspiring the name for this collection of resin figurines that can be posed. The Grizberg bear family and friends are indeed treasures with their moveable limbs and spiffy outfits. Three new pieces joined The Shoe Box Bears for Spring 2000. Each edition has 6,000 pieces.

DESK ANIMALS – Introduced in 1998, these ten not-quite ferocious, multi-piece animals look to be partly submerged in water. As their names imply, they are meant to be displayed on a desktop, computer or bookshelf. Wherever they "swim," these animals may bring a sense of wild whimsy to your work space.

BEARLY-BUILT VILLAGES – Boyds Town joined the Boyds resin collection in 2000 with a new series of buildings and accessories. Each of the six buildings feature removable roofs that reveal a detailed interior. The bottom-stamped, hand-numbered pieces comes in editions of 5,100 pieces.

Since the company's inception, each new offering has been enthusiastically received by collectors, resulting in the company's steady growth. By 1998, the company had become too large to run alone, so it was acquired by the investment firm of Kohlberg Kravis Roberts & Company. KKR and Boyds' president Bob Coccoluto have taken over the nitty-gritty business details, leaving "The Head Bean" with more time to devote to his creations, his fans and his family. The company's success was again obvious in 1999 with the creation of Boyds' first overseas sales subsidiary to expand the Boyds line in the United Kingdom and develop the line throughout Europe.

Collectors need not fear that all this expansion will take away the down-home feeling they have come to expect and love from Boyds. As long as Lowenthal is running the show, the wackiness, originality and genuine caring that has long characterized the company and the line is sure to continue.

Meet "The Head Bean"

There's no doubt about it. "The Head Bean Hisself," Gary M. Lowenthal, is a major part of the appeal of The Boyds Collection Ltd. His zany personality, warmth and genuine interest in his collectors make his appearances on QVC and at collectibles shows and signings wildly popular events. Here, some Boyds collectors share their experiences and thoughts, which help explain the Boyds phenomenon.

Jean from Connecticut has been collecting the Boyds line for nine years. "I just love Gary," she says. "He is as zany in person as he is on QVC." In the fall of 1999, Jean attended a signing at a store in Plainville, Connecticut. Her friend Joanne, who is also a big Gary fan, was unable to attend. So Jean brought a picture of her friend and asked Gary to hold it up so that she could take a photo of Joanne with Gary. "He did it willingly and also signed the picture for her," Jean says. "I can't wait until he comes back to Plainville for another signing! I'll be there! I also won one of the raffles that day, a signed resin "The Family" – it just doesn't get any better than this!"

Tami, a collector from Utah, and her two daughters met "The Head Bean" at a signing. "I was very impressed with Gary at the signing," she says. "He talked to each and every person and I could tell that he really liked the children."

Many Boyds collectors attend the International Collectibles Expositions in the hope of meeting Gary and getting a Boyds piece signed. Kathy from Illinois is one such person. She says she attends the Rosemont, Illinois, show every year and has met "The Head Bean" several times. She is impressed that Gary is so accessible to his collectors, "whether by being on QVC or meeting us at signings and

collectibles shows," she says. "Gary is so friendly with his collectors and he really, really listens to what you have to say." This willingness to listen is evidenced by his behavior at "The Head Bean Chat" at Rosemont. Kathy says Gary always gets the collector's opinion on various pieces, and asks for ideas on what to make next. She believes that Gary's company "really cares about their collectors."

Theresa from Michigan began collecting Boyds pieces in 1995. She and her husband went to the Rosemont collectibles show in 1998 where Gary signed her Boyds fifth anniversary piece,

"T.H.B.... Work Is Love Made Visible." She presented Gary with a special gift: a T-shirt emblazoned with the words "Dewey, Cheatem & Howe" and featuring a picture of the Three Stooges. "Since Gary is always saying 'get a-hold of my lawyers Dewey, Cheatem & Howe,' I had to give him the T-shirt! We all had a good laugh and Gary loved it," Theresa says. "Gary is very personable and takes the time to talk to each collector. He never hesitates to let you take pictures and is full of energy. He is genuinely interested in his collectors and has become friends with many of them. To sum it up in one word: TERRIFIC!"

Peggy from Kentucky met Gary at a signing in the fall of 1999. Peggy began collecting Boyds about five years ago and now has

more than 10,000 pieces in her collection. "I think Gary is a wonderful person and truly cares for people (even those who don't buy his bears.) He appreciates where he has been, where he is now, and is thankful for his loyal fans. You can tell him if you don't like something [about Boyds], and he listens. That is very important. Gary loves people, and he is loved back," she says. "I thank God every day for Gary and all the friends I have made through Boyds!"

California residents David and Sandi attended a signing in Chico, California, in 1998. "This was the only West Coast sign-

ing that year," says David. "If anyone there got bored, it was not Gary's fault. He made sure that there was not a dull moment [during] the entire event. Gary may well be the biggest ham of all time."

Iowa collector Julie is a dedicated Boyds fan who has met Gary at several signings and been impressed by each of those meetings. "He seems to have genuine concern about what we, the collectors, think," she says. "He really takes the time to listen to our thoughts and suggestions and will even ask *us* questions! I think that this really makes the collector feel a connection to Boyds that is unmatched in other collectible lines."

Although Elizabeth from Pennsylvania has never met Gary, she watches his television appearances on QVC. "I get a kick out of him," she says. "I think he adds the 'boy' to Boyds. He kind of reminds me of my two boys with his wacky sense of humor." Elizabeth is the proud owner of a wooden "Gnome Homes" sign from Gary's days in Boyds, Maryland. A local shopkeeper found the sign in the store's attic and gave it to Elizabeth, who displays it on top of a curio cabinet filled with Boyds resin figurines. "The sign is in perfect condition," she says. "I got a real kick out of it, since it is a piece of Gary's history."

What's New For Spring 2000

*T*his section highlights the new Boyds releases for Spring 2000, including pieces from The Purrstone Collection, a line introduced in 1999; The Garden Gang, a new subdivision of The Wee Folkstones; and the new Bearly-Built Villages series, which make their debut in 2000. New pieces exclusive to Canada are also featured in this section, proving that Boyds bears and hares are well traveled indeed.

The Bearstone Collection

GOODFER U. BEAR ... WAY TO GO! – This expressive bear can help convey your heartfelt pride for a job well done.

GREG MCBRUIN ... THE WIND UP – "Shoeless" Joe Jackson's got nothing on this guy, who soon may be shoeless himself if he doesn't watch out!

HUCK WITH MANDY, ZOE AND ZACK ... ROLLIN' ALONG – These three young cubs are in for a smooth ride on the "Bear Express."

IMA CHILLIN ... TAKIN' IT EASY – Basking in the sun, Ima appears to need no help in the relaxation department, despite the title of the book that is propped on her chest.

JONATHAN C. TOOTSENWHISTLE WITH MARJORIE MARCHALONG... ONE BEAR BAND (LE-2000) – No one can beat this one-bear band!

MOMMA & POPPA MCNEWBEAR WITH BABY BUNDLES – It's easy to see who is the center of attention in these new momma's and poppa's lives!

OL' MOTHER MCBEAR ... THE MORE THE MERRIER – This house, er, shoe, is filled to the brim with little cubs and a whole lot of love!

TILLIE HOPGOOD ... THE EGGSITTER – Although she'd rather be hopping through the forest, this hare takes her egg-sitting job seriously.

TWEEDLE BEDEEDLE ... STOP & SMELL THE FLOWERS – This wise "ladybug" offers a lesson we all should heed.

Noah's Pageant Series

HSING HSING AND LING LING WONGBRUIN ... CARRYOUT – These two pandas (and their food) are a welcome addition to Noah's Ark.

JOEY AND ALICE OUTBACK ... THE TREKKERS – Hop aboard Noah's Ark with this pair from the land "Down Under."

PACKY AND DERMAH TRUNKSPACE ... PACKIN' LITE – This *Noah's Pageant* pair have their trunks all packed and are ready for boarding.

WILLIE AS NOAH'S SON ... TOUGH JOB BUT ... SOMEBODY'S GOT TO DO IT! – Willie is more than up to the task, as long as his trusty frog comes along for the ride.

Other Bearstone Collectibles

ALEXANDRA AND BELLE ... TELEPHONE TIED – You're never more than a phone call away from the ones you love, as this charming frame suggests.

MOMMA & POPPA MCNEWBEAR WITH BABY BUNDLES – This new Bearstone musical makes a perfect gift for any proud momma or poppa!

ROSEMARIE AND EMMIE ... T.L.C. – This musical is one of the most recent additions to The Bearstone Collection.

 **LYDIA ... SHOWER OF ROSES** – Everything's coming up roses with this rustic – yet oh-so-elegant – votive candle holder.

TWEEDLE BEDEEDLE WITH LEEDLE AND COMPANY – This little "ladybug" and friend make delightful additions to any garden.

Bearwear Pins

 **BUZZBY BEE HAPPY** – It's easy to "bee happy" if you're wearing this Canadian exclusive pin on your lapel!

ARCHER ... STRAIGHTSHOT • **BABY BUNDLES** • **GREG MCBRUIN ... THE WINDUP** • **HUCK ... KEEP ON TRUCKIN'** • **IMA CHILLIN ... TAKIN' IT EASY** • **TWEEDLE BEDEEDLE ... STOP & SMELL THE FLOWERS** – Whether you're celebrating the love in your life, welcoming a new arrival, rooting for the home team or enjoying a quiet day by yourself, you can do it in style with a fashionable pin.

The Folkstone Collection

CALLIOPE CLIPSALOT WITH PINCHY ... GUARDIAN ANGEL OF PENNIES – This frugal angel reminds us that "a penny saved is a penny earned!"

Heather With Chris . . . Guardian Angel Of Volleyball – Set, spike, score! This angel provides inspiration for the champion in us all.

Honker T. Flatfoot . . . Send In The Clowns – No doubt about it. This winsome "clown" is bound to bring smiles to collectors everywhere.

Jack Hammer . . . Hard Hat – This hard-working construction bear is ready for any job that might come his way!

Momma McHutch And Babies . . . Family Matters – This mother may be "hare-ied," but she knows that it's the family that makes the world go round.

Sam, Libby And Ellis . . . Fife And Drum (LE-2000) – This patriotic trio is "proud to serve," but its time is limited so take it home while you can!

Solstice Angeldance . . . Sunlight – Brighten someone's day with this sunny angel from The Folkstone Collection.

Carvers Choice

Maribel Moonbeam . . . Top Of The Moon (LE-2000) – This cow is an out-of-this-world addition to the Carvers Choice family.

MERINO WOOLMORE AND CHAUNCEY . . . THE SPEEDSTERS (LE-2000) – They might not be the fastest pair, but this sheep and snail will race right into your heart.

PERCY TUNABREATH . . . GOT FISH? (LE-2000) – This kitty went fishin' for his dinner, but the catch of the day is not quite what he had in mind.

SHY BESSIE BOVINE . . . FRESH FROM THE PASTURE (LE-2000) – This bashful bovine brings a fragrant touch to the *Carvers Choice* line.

UNCLE SAMMY LEGHORN AND GEORGE . . . ROLLING ALONG (LE-2000) – What a patriotic pair this rooster and inchworm are!

WILMA QUACKSWORTH WITH FELIX AND FRED . . . RIDIN' HIGH (LE-2000) – This bear feels like he's riding on top of the world!

The Wee Folkstones

AMBER FAERIEDREAMS . . . DEEP IN THE FOREST – This Wee Folkstone fairy is sure to bring you sweet dreams.

MARY ANGELWISH . . . MAY YOUR WISHES ALL COME TRUE – Birthday wishes are being granted by this adorable little angel.

POLLY PEKOE ... A SIP OF TEA – Take a break from your busy day and make time for a nice, soothing cup of tea with Polly.

SUDSIE FAERIESOCK ... MISCHIEF MAKER – Could this little lady be the sock-stealing imp who lurks in laundry rooms everywhere?

The Wee Folkstones ... The Garden Gang

FARMER MCHARE ... BEST INTENTIONS – This little fella' from the new *Garden Gang* series appeals to the lazybones in all of us.

MOMMA MCHOPPLE AND BABIES ... NAPTIME – Shhh! It's naptime in the garden!

The Wee Folkstones ... Ribbit & Co.

JEBEDIAH PUDDLEJUMP ... WHAT A DRIP! – Dressed in his yellow slicker, this *Ribbit & Co.* frog is ready for some serious splashing!

LLOYD TADPOOL ... SURF'S UP – Splish, splash, this tiny tadpole is taking a bath.

PRINCESS PUCKERUP . . . KISS ME QUICK! – In a new twist on an old fairy tale, this frog princess seeks to turn a prince into a frog!

Other Folkstone Collectibles

WENDY WILLOWHARE . . . A TISKET A TASKET – This Folkstone frame will bring a dash of country charm to any setting.

CAFFEINATA "SPEEDY" P. FAERIEBEAN – This fairy sits atop a canister of coffee beans in this musical piece.

LIDDY PEARL – Bears, bees and blossoms adorn this special votive holder from The Folkstone Collection.

Folkwear Pins

CALLIOPE CLIPSALOT . . . GUARDIAN ANGEL OF PENNIES • CHESTER BIRDBREATH . . . WHAT BIRD? • HEATHER . . . GUARDIAN ANGEL OF VOLLEYBALL • HONKER T. FLATFOOT . . . SEND IN THE CLOWNS • JEBEDIAH PUDDLEJUMP . . . WHAT A DRIP! • PRINCESS PUCKERUP . . . KISS ME QUICK! – Express yourself the Boyds way – with wit, humor and just a touch of zaniness.

The Purrstone Collection

CHESTER BIRDBREATH... WHAT BIRD? – This Purrstone kitty is trying to cover up his misdeeds, without much success.

DOMINIQUE SUREFOOT WITH COACH COLBY . . . PRACTICE MAKES PURRFECT – This little lady is a "purrfect" ten in any collector's book!

KANDACE PURRSHOP . . . HIDDEN SURPRISES – Well, isn't this a surprise! The Easter Bunny is really an Easter Kitty!

MAMA PURRSMORE AND BABY BELLE WITH RINKY, DINKY AND DEW . . . ONCE UPON A TIME – A good book brings everyone together.

NADIA SUREFOOT WITH COACH MUENSTER – This Canadian exclusive features a champion cat performing a delicate balancing act.

OPIE BAITHOOK WITH BARNEY . . . CATCH OF THE DAY – These two pals are relaxing at their favorite fishin' hole.

POKIE PAWSWORTHY . . . THE BUG INSPECTOR – Cats love to poke at bugs, and this curious feline is no exception.

Yesterday's Child
The Dollstone Collection

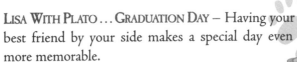

BARBARA ANN WITH JODI AND ANNIE . . . STITCHED WITH LOVE – This merry trio is new from The Dollstone Collection.

BROOKE WITH JOSHUA . . . PUDDLE JUMPERS – What could be more fun than splashing around with your best buddy?

CASEY WITH BAXTER . . . AFTERNOON STROLL (LE-2000) – Playing "Mommy" is a lot of fun with a "baby" as cute as Baxter!

CINDY WITH COLLIER . . . DRESS UP – Collier is just delighted to sit still while her friend adds a pretty pink ribbon to her fur.

LISA WITH PLATO . . . GRADUATION DAY – Having your best friend by your side makes a special day even more memorable.

MICHAEL AND THAYER . . . WAITIN' FOR GRANDPA – Grandpa is mighty special – he always has time for his favorite fishin' buddies.

RYAN & DIANE WITH CORY, WESLEY AND CARLY . . . LOVE IS FOREVER – These bears (and hare) wouldn't miss this day for the world.

Other Dollstone Collectibles

MIRANDA AND ROBERT ... PUT ON A HAPPY FACE – A young lady's favorite pastime is celebrated in this nostalgic musical.

KELLY AND COMPANY ... THE BEAR COLLECTOR – This beautiful Dollstone waterglobe is filled with the "bear" necessities.

Yesterday's Child ... The Doll Collection

ALYSSA WITH CAROLINE & CARLA ... A STITCH IN TIME (LE-18,000, G.M.'S CHOICE) – This 16" limited edition porcelain doll is a timeless beauty.

EMILEE WITH OTIS ... FOREVER – This 12" porcelain doll is ready for her big day because she knows that her love will last forever.

ERICA WITH FERRIS ... CARNIVAL FUN – Erica is an open edition doll who'll be happy to share her cotton candy with you!

ERIN LYNN WITH SQUIRT ... PEPPERMINT LEMONADE (LE-12,000) – This unusual flavor tastes mighty sweet when you have someone to share it with.

JONI WITH PATCH ... STRAWBERRY FIELDS – Don't worry, this little gal certainly has enough strawberry kisses for everyone.

LEAH WITH WINDY ... SUMMER BREEZE – A pinwheel and a special pal make any summer day fun.

LUCINDA WITH GILLIGAN ... BY THE SEA (LE-12,000) – These two are having buckets of fun!

MOLLY WITH CRICKET ... WINGED FRIENDS (LE-12,000) – As you can see by her necklace, Molly loves her flying friends.

NICOLE WITH BUZZ ... SWEETER THAN HONEY (LE-12,000) – Buzz thinks some honey would indeed be quite yummy in his tummy.

REBECCA WITH ELLIOT ... BIRTHDAY (LE-12,000) – What a special day for this exquisite doll and her teddy!

TAYLOR WITH JUMPER ... PLAY TIME (LE-12,000) – Play time is definitely the best time, as Taylor and Jumper well know.

The Shoe Box Bears

CHICKLET GRIZBERG ... A SPRINKLE IN TIME – This Shoe Box Bear is all ready for spring in his baby chick costume.

PADDY O'BEARY ... LUCK OF THE IRISH – It's St. Patrick's Day all year round for this lucky Irish bear!

WEBSTER GRIZBERG ... JUST DUCKIE – Webster hopes to paddle his way into your heart and home with his offering of flowers.

Bearly-Built Villages

BAILEY'S COZY COTTAGE · THE BOYDS BEARLY A SCHOOL · THE CHAPEL IN THE WOODS · EDMUND'S HIDEAWAY · PUBLIC LIBEARY · TED E. BEAR SHOP – Boyds bears and friends celebrate the birth of Boyds Town with six intricately-carved buildings and accessory sets.

Coming Soon!

SAN FRANCISCO MUSIC BOX MUSICALS –

Bud Buzzby Honey Bee (#2789SF, "*Here Comes The Sun*")
By The Sea (#2790SF, "*Those Were The Days*")
Learn To Be Happy (#2794SF, "*I'd Like To Teach The World To Sing*")
Shipmates (#2788SF, "*Up A Lazy River*")
Sissie & Squirt ... Big Helper (#2792SF, "*Help*")
Slugger (#2793SF, "*Take Me Out To The Ball Game*")
Stitch In Time (#2791SF, "*Love Makes The World Go Round*")

Club News

*I*f you enjoyed last year's Loyal Order of Friends of Boyds "Bloomin' F.o.B." flower theme, then you'll love what "The Head Bean" has cooked up (literally) for the year 2000. This year's "Brewin' F.o.B" tea party theme is based on a poem that inspired Catherine and Caitlin Berriweather to imbibe in a cup of tea. Each club kit comes with a copy of this poem, which can be framed and displayed with your club pieces.

For an annual membership fee of $32.50, collectors will receive the following gifts:

CATHERINE AND CAITLIN BERRIWEATHER . . . FINE CUP OF TEA – This Bearstone Collection figurine finds mother and daughter enjoying the togetherness of tea time.

CAITLIN BERRIWEATHER – This beautiful 6" plush bear, who loves poetry as well as a good cup of tea, sports a navy blue and cream-colored checkered chenille vest with a smart navy blue bonnet.

CAITLIN BERRIWEATHER – This Bearwear™ Pin, which can be displayed or worn on your lapel, features Caitlin savoring a cup of tea.

BREWIN' F.O.B. MINI-TEA SET – This beautiful little tea pot with three cups and saucers – all decorated with Boyds' signature bear paw print – is available to club members who join the club for an extra $7.50 fee.

In addition, all club members receive a one-year subscription to *The Boyds F.o.B. Bear Inquirer*. Written by "The Head Bean Hisself," this newsletter comes out four times a year and keeps members up to date on what's happening in the world of Boyds.

Club members also have the opportunity to purchase exclusive Members Only pieces throughout the year. This year, members have the opportunity to buy pieces to complete the tea party motif:

CATHERINE BERRIWEATHER AND LITTLE SCRUFF – These 11" and 3" plush dolls (respectively) can complete your "Tea For Three" theme that started with the plush membership gift "Caitlin Berriweather."

CATHERINE AND CAITLIN BERRIWEATHER WITH LITTLE SCRUFF . . . FAMILY TRADITIONS – This resin figurine brings all three members of the "tea party" together in one grouping.

NOAH'S TOOL BOX – This year, club members will also have the opportunity to purchase an exclusive 2" tall tool chest that complements the *Noah's Pageant Series* pieces.

The Loyal Order of Friends of Boyds (F.o.B. for short), a club exclusively for Boyds fans, was established in 1996 due to popular demand. Each year, members have been treated to a special theme, and the club gifts include both resin and plush pieces.

To join the club, check with your retailer or fill out the application form in the back of this Collector's Value Guide™. Mail the application with the appropriate payment ($32.50 for a basic membership, or $40 to also receive this year's "Brewin' F.o.B. Mini-Tea Set") to:

THE BOYDS COLLECTION LTD.
P.O. BOX 4386 F.O.B. DEPT.
GETTYSBURG, PA 17325-4386

Spotlight On
Other Boyds Products

O f course the Boyds resin figurines occupy a treasured place in your heart and home, but do you know about the other great lines that make up The Boyds Collection Ltd.?

BOYDS PLUSH ANIMALS – The Boyds Collection Ltd. features more than 1,000 plush animals in its menagerie, with more delightful friends joining the clan each year. In 1999, Boyds artist Gary M. Lowenthal introduced an adorable group of plush penguins into the family, an occasion he celebrated by appearing dressed as a penguin in the fall on the popular Boyds QVC television show. The Boyds bears, in all their many forms, remain the most populous critters, but there is also a sizeable army of hares, dogs, cats and even frogs, elephants, pigs and moose!

ACCESSORIES – Because Boyds plush animals are such an important part of the Boyds family, collectors can make their animals feel truly at home with accessories from *The Bear Necessities* line. These items include cozy sweaters and fashionable dresses for your plush pals (some critters arrive "bear nekked," after all), as well as a variety of quilts, furniture, eye glasses and even kitchenware (so your busy bears can whip up a "dee-lect-able" dessert!)

ORNAMENTS – Decorate to the hilt with more than 60 ornaments from the Boyds collection. With critters ranging from bears and hares (some of whom even come in pairs!) to antique dolls and angelic kitties, there's no limit to the decorating possibilities. These soft and cuddly ornaments are sure to bring the warmth and spirit of the holidays to your hearth and home.

BOXES – Boyds offers two porcelain box collections that are perfect for holding (or hiding) your little treasures. Le Bearmoge Collection features your favorite bears atop exquisite porcelain boxes, each with a miniature figure inside to serve as guardian of your goods. The Beatrice Collection, named for "The Head Bean's" mother, consist of a line of hinged porcelain boxes that are reproduced from hand painted originals. Each one comes with a heart-felt sentiment painted on the interior.

BEARWARE POTTERYWORKS – Salt and pepper shakers, cookie jars and mugs make up the bulk of the Bearware Potteryworks collection of human-sized kitchen accessories, introduced in 1997. If you can't get enough Boyds creations, these shiny, glazed ceramic pieces may just be the perfect addition to your collection.

Bearstones Top Ten

his section showcases the ten most valuable pieces in The Bearstone Collection based on 2000 secondary market values. Each piece has significantly increased in value from its original retail price, as shown by our Market Meter.

CHRISTMAS BEAR ELF WITH LIST (#BC2051)
Issued: 1994 • Retired: 1994
Secondary Market Value: 1E • $1,300
Original Price: $24.99 (Can.)
Market Meter: + 6,223%

GRENVILLE … WITH GREEN SCARF (#2003-04)
Issued: 1993 • Retired: 1993
Secondary Market Value: 1E • $650
Original Price: $11
Market Meter: +5,809%

WILSON WITH LOVE SONNETS (#2007)
Issued: 1993 • Retired: 1997
Secondary Market Value: 1E • $625
Original Price: $13
Market Meter: +4,708%

GRENVILLE THE SANTABEAR (#2030)
Issued: 1994 • Retired: 1996
Secondary Market Value: 1E • $585
Original Price: $14.50
Market Meter: +3,934%

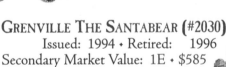

BAILEY BEAR WITH SUITCASE (#2000)
Issued: 1993 • Current
Secondary Market Value: 1E • $575
Original Price: $14.50
Market Meter: +3,866%

FATHER CHRISBEAR AND SON (#2008)
Issued: 1993 • Retired: 1993
Secondary Market Value: 1E • $495
Original Price: $14.50
Market Meter: + 3,314%

GRENVILLE & BEATRICE . . . BEST FRIENDS
(#2016. DOVE ON RIGHT SIDE OF BASE)
Issued: 1994 • Retired: 1999
Secondary Market Value: 1E • $490
Original Price: $26
Market Meter: + 1,785%

CLARA . . . THE NURSE
(#2231, ORIGINAL VERSION)
Issued: 1994 • Retired: 1998
Secondary Market Value: 1E • $460
Original Price: $16
Market Meter: + 2,775%

SIMONE DE BEARVOIRE & HER MOM,
MY AUNTIE ALICE
(#2001, NO PATCHES ON PAWS)
Issued: 1993 • Retired: 1996
Secondary Market Value: 1E• $420
Original Price: $14.50
Market Meter: + 2,797%

CELESTE . . . THE ANGEL RABBIT (#2230)
Issued: 1994 • Retired: 1997
Secondary Market Value: 1E • $375
Original Price: $16.50
Market Meter: + 2,173%

Folkstones Top Five

his section lists the five most valuable pieces in The Folkstone Collection as determined by their 2000 values on the secondary market. Each piece has significantly increased in value from its original retail price, as shown by our Market Meter.

ETHERAL . . . ANGEL OF LIGHT
(LE-7,200, #28203-06)
Issued: 1996 • Retired: 1996
Secondary Market Value: NE • $189
Original Price: $19
Market Meter: + 895%

NA-NICK AND SIEGFRIED . . .
THE PLAN (LE-10,000, #2807)
Issued: 1996 • Retired: 1996
Secondary Market Value: NE • $165
Original Price: $34
Market Meter: + 385%

DECEMBER 26TH
(*SANTA & FRIENDS*, #3003)
Issued: 1996 • Retired: 1997
Secondary Market Value: 1E • $130
Original Price: $33
Market Meter: + 294%

NICK ON ICE
(*SANTA & FRIENDS*, #3001, ORIGINAL VERSION)
Issued: 1994 • Retired: 1997
Secondary Market Value: 1E • $125
Original Price: $33
Market Meter: + 279%

JINGLE MOOSE (#2830, ORIGINAL VERSION)
Issued: 1994 • Retired: 1996
Secondary Market Value: 1E • $123
Original Price: $16
Market Meter: + 669%

Dollstones Top Five

*T*his section highlights the five most valuable pieces in The Dollstone Collection based upon 2000 secondary market values. Each piece shows a significant increase in value from its original retail price, as shown by our Market Meter.

JENNIFER WITH PRISCILLA . . .
THE DOLL IN THE ATTIC (#3500)
Issued: 1996 ♦ Retired: 1997
Secondary Market Value: PR ♦ $225
Original Price: $20.50
Market Meter: +998%

PATRICIA WITH MOLLY . . .
ATTIC TREASURES (#3501)
Issued: 1996 ♦ Retired: 1999
Secondary Market Value: PR ♦ $220
Original Price: $14
Market Meter: +1,471%

KATHERINE WITH EDMUND & AMANDA . . .
KIND HEARTS (#3505)
Issued: 1996 ♦ Current
Secondary Market Value: PR ♦ $175
Original Price: $20
Market Meter: +775%

MALLORY WITH PATSY & J.B. BEAN . . .
TRICK OR TREAT (#3517)
Issued: 1996 ♦ Current
Secondary Market Value: PR ♦ $170
Original Price: $27
Market Meter: +530%

SARAH & HEATHER WITH ELLIOT, DOLLY
& AMELIA . . . TEA FOR FOUR (#3507)
Issued: 1996 ♦ Retired: 1996
Secondary Market Value: PR ♦ $170
Original Price: $47
Market Meter: +257%

Future Retirements

*B*oyds has announced that it plans to retire the following pieces by December 31, 2000, giving collectors time to purchase these pieces before they become hard to find. Each piece's issue year and item number appears in parenthesis after its name.

The Bearstone Collection

GENERAL FIGURINES
Jonathan C. Tootsenwhistle With Marjorie Marchalong . . . One Bear Band (2000, #227806)

FRAMES
The Collector (1998, #27301)

MUSICALS
Ms. Bruin & Bailey . . . The Lesson (1999, #270554)

VOTIVE HOLDERS
Bailey & Huck . . . Wheee!!! (1998, #27752)
Ms. Bruin & Bailey . . . Tea Time (1997, #27751)

The Folkstone Collection

GENERAL FIGURINES
Dr. R.X. Mooselberry . . . Making Rounds (1999, #28301)
Francoise & Suzanne . . . The Spree (1998, #2875)
I.B. Coldman . . . Ice Is Nice (1998, #28102)
Luna . . . By The Light Of The Silvery Moon (1998, #28207)
Polaris And The North Star . . . On Ice (1997, #2880)
Prudence . . . Daffodils (1997, #2847)
Sam, Libby And Ellis . . . Fife And Drum (2000, #2886)

CARVERS CHOICE
Maribel Moonbeam . . . Top Of The Moon (2000, #370055)
Merino Woolmore And Chauncey . . . The Speedsters (2000, #370056)
Percy Tunabreath . . . Got Fish? (2000, #370060)
Shy Bessie Bovine . . . Fresh From The Pasture (2000, #370058)
Uncle Sammy Leghorn And George . . . Rolling Along (2000, #370057)
Wilma Quacksworth With Felix and Fred . . . Ridin' High (2000, #370059)

THE WEE FOLKSTONES
Indulgenia Q. Bluit . . . Angel Of Denial (1998, #36305)

MUSICALS
Cocoa M. Angelrich And Scoop (1999, #271050, *The Wee Folkstones*)

WATERGLOBES
Ms. McFrazzle . . . On The Job (1999, #271002)

The Dollstone Collection

GENERAL FIGURINES
Benjamin With Matthew . . . The Speed Trap (1997, #3524)
Betsy With Edmund . . . The Patriots (1996, #3503)
Casey With Baxter . . . Afternoon Stroll (2000, #3557)
Laura With Jane . . . First Day Of School (1997, #3522)
Mark With Luke . . . The Prayer (1999, #3545)
Rebecca With Elliot . . . Birthday (1996, #3509)
Shelby . . . Asleep In Teddy's Arms (1998, #3527)
Tami With Doug . . . Half Time (1999, #3546)

FRAMES
Laura With Jane . . . First Day Of School (1999, #27552)
Tiffany . . . "Forever" (1998, #27550)

VOTIVE HOLDERS
Candice With Matthew . . . Gathering Apples (1999, #27901)

Yesterday's Child . . . The Doll Collection

PORCELAIN DOLLS
Alyssa With Caroline & Carla . . . A Stitch In Time (2000, #4928)
Lucinda With Gilligan . . . By The Sea (2000, #4929)
Molly With Cricket . . . Winged Friends (2000, #4924)
Nicole With Buzz . . . Sweeter Than Honey (2000, #4925)
Rebecca With Elliot . . . Birthday (2000, #4927)
Taylor With Jumper . . . Play Time (2000, #4926)

The Shoe Box Bears

GENERAL FIGURINES
Ellie Grizberg . . . Egg Hunter (1999, #3212)
Momma Grizberg . . . Egg Decorator (1999, #3211)
Winnie Hopkins & Bunnylove (1998, #3207)

How To Use
The Collector's Value Guide™

1. Locate your piece in the Value Guide, which is in the following order: Bearstones, Folkstones, Purrstones, Dollstones, porcelain dolls, Shoe Box Bears, DeskAnimals, Bearly-Built Villages and the collector's club pieces. Within each section, figurines are listed first, followed by an alphabetical listing of miscellaneous items, such as music boxes and ornaments. To quickly locate a piece, refer to the Bearfinder indexes beginning on page 227.

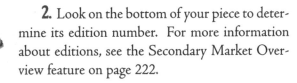

2. Look on the bottom of your piece to determine its edition number. For more information about editions, see the Secondary Market Overview feature on page 222.

3. Find the market value of your piece, based on its edition (such as 1E, 2E and 3E). For current pieces, the "AE" value is listed as the approximate current retail price. The key at the bottom of this page explains the abbreviations used in the Value Guide. For more information about variations, refer to the Variations feature on page 219.

4. Record in pencil both the original price that you paid and the current value of the piece, according to the edition number, in the corresponding box at the bottom of each page. Then, calculate the total value for the entire page.

5. Transfer the totals from each page to the Total Value Of My Collection worksheets beginning on page 216. Add all the totals together to determine the overall value of your collection.

SECONDARY MARKET VALUES KEY

AE = all editions 4E and higher
N/A = value is not applicable; no such edition number exists
NE = a piece has no edition number, only one market value
N/E = secondary market value has yet to be established
PR = QVC Premier Edition

General Figurines

Nine new pieces bring the total number of Bearstone figurines to 153. These new Bearstones include a limited edition piece, as well as the resin figurine "Ol' Mother McBear . . . The More The Merrier," the first release in the new *Classic Beary Tales* series.

	Values
1E	$38
2E	$26
3E	$20
AE	$16.50

**Ada Mae Cherries Jubilee . . .
Life Is A Bowl Of Cherries**
(Parade Of Gifts Exclusive)
#227723POG • Original Price: $16.50
Issued: 1999 • Current

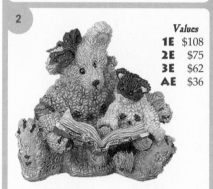

	Values
1E	$108
2E	$75
3E	$62
AE	$36

Agatha & Shelly . . . "Scaredy Cat"
#2246 • Original Price: $14.50
Issued: 1994 • Retired: 1998

	Values
1E	$45
2E	$38
3E	$29
AE	$19

**Alexandra And Belle . . .
Telephone Tied**
#227720 • Original Price: $19
Issued: 1999 • Current

	Values
1E	$45
2E	$26
3E	$26
AE	$26

**Alexis Bearinsky . . .
The Night Before Christmas**
#228314 • Original Price: $26
Issued: 1999 • Current

General Figurines		
Date Purchased	Price Paid	Value
1.		
2.		
3.		
4.		
Totals		

1

Value
NE $43

Alexis Bearinsky…
Twas The Night Before Christmas
(GCC Early Release)
#228314GCC • Original Price: $24.50
Issued: 1998 • Retired: 1998

2

Values
1E $90
2E $68
3E $55
AE $33

Amelia's Enterprise…Carrot Juice
#2258 • Original Price: $16.50
Issued: 1995 • Retired: 1998

3

Values
1E $76
2E $55
3E $44
AE $28

Angelica…The Guardian
#2266 • Original Price: $18.50
Issued: 1995 • Retired: 1999

4

Values
1E $50
2E $42
3E $35
AE $21
Variation
NE $55

Arnold P. Bomber…The Duffer
#227714 • Original Price: $21
Issued: 1999 • Current
Variation: 1998 GCC Early Release

General Figurines

	Date Purchased	Price Paid	Value
1.			
2.			
3.			
4.			
5.			
	Totals		

5

Values
1E $185
2E $152
3E $124
AE $98

Arthur…With Red Scarf
#2003-03 • Original Price: $11
Issued: 1993 • Retired: 1994

The Bearstone Collection

1

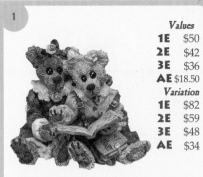

Values	
1E	$50
2E	$42
3E	$36
AE	$18.50
Variation	
1E	$82
2E	$59
3E	$48
AE	$34

Bailey & Becky ... The Diary (RS)
#228304 • Original Price: $18.50
Issued: 1997 • Current
Variation: original version

2

Values	
1E	$175
2E	$114
3E	$98
AE	$80

Bailey & Emily ... Forever Friends
#2018 • Original Price: $34
Issued: 1994 • Retired: 1996

3

Values	
1E	$335
2E	$205
3E	$150
AE	$60

TO HAVE AND TO HOLD

Bailey & Wixie ... To Have And To Hold
#2017 • Original Price: $16
Issued: 1994 • Retired: 1998

4

Values	
1E	$188
2E	$155
3E	$125
AE	$90

Bailey At The Beach
#2020-09 • Original Price: $16
Issued: 1994 • Retired: 1995

5

Values	
1E	$575
2E	$370
3E	$275
AE	$14.50
Variation	
1E	$156
2E	N/A
3E	N/A
AE	N/A

Bailey Bear With Suitcase
#2000 • Original Price: $14.50
Issued: 1993 • Current
Variation: smooth fur, brown bottom

General Figurines

	Date Purchased	Price Paid	Value
1.			
2.			
3.			
4.			
5.			
	Totals		

Value Guide — Boyds Bears & Friends™

1

Values	
1E	$105
2E	$68
3E	$55
AE	$15

Bailey ... Heart's Desire
#2272 • Original Price: $15
Issued: 1996 • Current

2

Values	
1E	N/A
2E	N/A
3E	N/A
AE	$63
Variation	
1E	$325
2E	$210
3E	$168
AE	$82

Bailey ... In The Orchard
#2006 • Original Price: $14.50
Issued: 1993 • Retired: 1996
Variation: paw print on jug

3

Values	
1E	$95
2E	$79
3E	$64
AE	$48

Bailey ... Poor Ol' Bear
#227704 • Original Price: $15
Issued: 1997 • Retired: 1997

4

Values	
1E	$60
2E	$33
3E	$25
AE	$13
Variation 1	
1E	$98
2E	$70
3E	$57
AE	$26
Variation 2	
1E	$325

Bailey The Baker With Sweetie Pie (RS)
#2254 • Original Price: $13
Issued: 1995 • Current
Variation 1: original version
Variation 2: "Clarion Bear"

General Figurines

	Date Purchased	Price Paid	Value
1.			
2.			
3.			
4.			

Totals

1

Values	
1E	$45
2E	$38
3E	$32
AE	$18
Variation	
NE	$48

Bailey ... The Bride
#227712 • Original Price: $18
Issued: 1999 • Current
Variation: 1998 GCC Early Release
"Bailey ... As The Bride"

2

Values	
1E	$70
2E	$55
3E	$45
AE	$16

Bailey ... The Cheerleader
#2268 • Original Price: $16
Issued: 1995 • Current

3

Values	
1E	$45
2E	$36
3E	$30
AE	$17
Variation	
1E	$57
2E	$40
3E	$33
AE	$27

Bailey ... The Graduate – Carpe Diem (RS)
#227701-10 • Original Price: $17
Issued: 1997 • Current
Variation: original version

4

Values	
1E	$95
2E	$72
3E	$56
AE	$16

Bailey The Honey Bear
#2260 • Original Price: $16
Issued: 1995 • Current

5

Values	
1E	$280
2E	$165
3E	$125
AE	$42

Bailey's Birthday
#2014 • Original Price: $16
Issued: 1994 • Retired: 1999

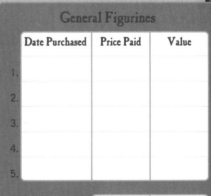

General Figurines

	Date Purchased	Price Paid	Value
1.			
2.			
3.			
4.			
5.			

Totals

41

The Bearstone Collection®

1

Values	
JAN	$115
FEB	$85
MAR	$72
APR-DEC	$62

Beatrice...We Are Always The Same Age Inside (LE-1998)
#227802 • Original Price: $48
Issued: 1998 • Retired: 1998

2

Value	
NE	$35
Variation	
NE	N/E

Bee My Honey
(LE-19,487, Parade Of Gifts Exclusive)
#94575POG • Original Price: $12
Issued: 1998 • Retired: 1998
Variation: "Larade of Gifts" bottomstamp

3

Values	
1E	$114
2E	$84
3E	$70
AE	$55

Bessie The Santa Cow
#2239 • Original Price: $16
Issued: 1994 • Retired: 1996

4

Values	
1E	$42
2E	$35
3E	$24
AE	$16

Bumble B. Bee... Sweeter Than Honey
#227718 • Original Price: $16
Issued: 1999 • Current

General Figurines

	Date Purchased	Price Paid	Value
1.			
2.			
3.			
4.			
5.			

Totals

5

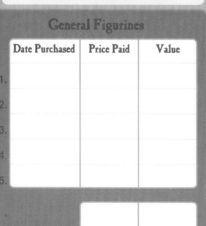

Values	
1E	$56
2E	$40
3E	$34
AE	$18

Buzz...The Flash
#227706 • Original Price: $18
Issued: 1997 • Current

1

Values	
1E	N/A
2E	N/A
3E	N/A
AE	$110
Variation	
1E	$165
2E	$115
3E	$108
AE	N/A

Byron & Chedda With Catmint
#2010 • Original Price: $14.50
Issued: 1993 • Retired: 1994
Variation: no patches on left arm

2

Value	
NE	$36

Caren B. Bearlove (GCC Exclusive)
#227722GCC • Original Price: $13.50
Issued: 1999 • Retired: 1999

3

Values	
1E	$375
2E	$250
3E	$200
AE	$80

Celeste … The Angel Rabbit
#2230 • Original Price: $16.50
Issued: 1994 • Retired: 1997

4

Values	
JAN	$90
FEB	$82
MAR	$70
APR-DEC	$62

Chandler, Mercy, Felicity Constance, Faith, Y.K. & Tew … Light A Candle For A Brighter World (Bearstone Millennium, LE)
#227805 • Original Price: $53
Issued: 1999 • Retired: 1999

5

Values	
1E	$127
2E	$90
3E	$75
AE	$57

Charlotte & Bebe … The Gardeners
#2229 • Original Price: $16
Issued: 1994 • Retired: 1995

General Figurines

	Date Purchased	Price Paid	Value
1.			
2.			
3.			
4.			
5.			
	Totals		

43

The Bearstone Collection

1

Values (U.S.)	
1E	$75
2E	$58
3E	$46
AE	$38

Chelsea Kainada ... The Practice
(LE-1997, Canadian Exclusive)
#BC22851 • Original Price: $29.99 (Can.)
Issued: 1997 • Retired: 1997

2

Values	
1E	$42
2E	$30
3E	$22
AE	$17

Chrissie ... Game, Set, Match
#227717 • Original Price: $17
Issued: 1999 • Current

3

Values	
1E	$155
2E	$102
3E	$85
AE	$48

Christian By The Sea
#2012 • Original Price: $14.50
Issued: 1993 • Retired: 1998

4

Values (U.S.)	
1E	$1300
2E	N/A
3E	N/A
AE	N/A

Christmas Bear Elf With List
(LE-1,872, Canadian Exclusive)
#BC2051 • Original Price: $24.99(Can.)
Issued: 1994 • Retired: 1994

General Figurines

	Date Purchased	Price Paid	Value
1.			
2.			
3.			
4.			
5.			

Totals

5

Values	
1E	N/A
2E	N/A
3E	N/A
AE	$40
Variation	
1E	$460
2E	$295
3E	$250
AE	$52

Clara ... The Nurse (RS)
#2231 • Original Price: $16
Issued: 1994 • Retired: 1998
Variation: original version

1

Values	
1E	$150
2E	$100
3E	$82
AE	$60

Clarence Angel Bear
#2029-11 • Original Price: $13
Issued: 1994 • Retired: 1995

2

Values	
1E	$45
2E	$38
3E	$33
AE	$21
Variation 1	
NE	$58
Variation 2	
1E	$75
2E	$43
3E	$56
AE	$30

The Collector (RS)
#227707 • Original Price: $21
Issued: 1998 • Current
Variation 1: 1997 GCC Early Release
Variation 2: original version

3

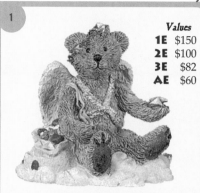

Values	
1E	$82
2E	$62
3E	$55
AE	$34

Cookie Catberg ... Knittin' Kitten
#2250 • Original Price: $19
Issued: 1995 • Retired: 1997

4

Values	
1E	$105
2E	$77
3E	$64
AE	$50

Cookie The Santa Cat
#2237 • Original Price: $15.50
Issued: 1994 • Retired: 1995

5

Values	
1E	$100
2E	$65
3E	$52
AE	$36

Daphne & Eloise ... Women's Work
#2251 • Original Price: $18
Issued: 1995 • Retired: 1999

General Figurines

	Date Purchased	Price Paid	Value
1.			
2.			
3.			
4.			
5.			
		Totals	

The Bearstone Collection

1

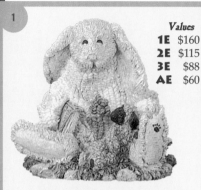

Values	
1E	$160
2E	$115
3E	$88
AE	$60

Daphne Hare & Maisey Ewe
#2011 • Original Price: $14.50
Issued: 1993 • Retired: 1995

2

Values	
1E	$170
2E	$125
3E	$100
AE	$48

Daphne … The Reader Hare
#2226 • Original Price: $14.50
Issued: 1994 • Retired: 1998

3

Value	
NE	$50

Dean Newbearger III …
Bears & Bulls (GCC Exclusive)
#227715GCC • Original Price: $16
Issued: 1998 • Retired: 1998

4

Values	
1E	$53
2E	$42
3E	$36
AE	$15

Dr. Harrison Griz …
M.D., Ph.D., B.U.D.
#228309 • Original Price: $15
Issued: 1998 • Current

General Figurines

	Date Purchased	Price Paid	Value
1.			
2.			
3.			
4.			

Totals

Value Guide — Boyds Bears & Friends™

1

Values	
1E	$92
2E	$55
3E	$39
AE	$14

Eddie ... Proud To Be A Bearmerican
#228312 • Original Price: $14
Issued: 1998 • Current

2

Values	
1E	$199
2E	$115
3E	$88
AE	$24

Edmund & Bailey ... Gathering Holly
#2240 • Original Price: $24
Issued: 1994 • Current

3

Values	
1E	$55
2E	$42
3E	$34
AE	$15

Edmund The Elf ... The Christmas Carol
#228311 • Original Price: $15
Issued: 1998 • Current

4

Values	
1E	$42
2E	$33
3E	$29
AE	$17
Variation	
1E	$60
2E	$44
3E	$34
AE	$26

Edmund ... The Graduate — Carpe Diem (RS)
#227701-07 • Original Price: $17
Issued: 1997 • Current
Variation: original version

5

Values	
1E	$114
2E	$86
3E	$62
AE	$55

Elgin The Elf Bear
#2236 • Original Price: $14.50
Issued: 1994 • Retired: 1997

General Figurines

	Date Purchased	Price Paid	Value
1.			
2.			
3.			
4.			
5.			
	Totals		

1

Value
NE $65

Elizabeth ... I <u>Am</u> The Queen
(LE-1998, Special Event Piece)
#01998-71 • Original Price: $35
Issued: 1998 • Retired: 1998

2

Values
1E $125
2E $94
3E $75
AE $49

Elliot & Snowbeary
#2242 • Original Price: $15.50
Issued: 1994 • Retired: 1999

3

Values
1E $280
2E $165
3E $125
AE $37

Elliot & The Tree
#2241 • Original Price: $16.50
Issued: 1994 • Retired: 1999

4

Values
1E $95
2E $67
3E $50
AE $17

Elliot ... The Hero
#2280 • Original Price: $17
Issued: 1996 • Current

General Figurines

Date Purchased	Price Paid	Value
1.		
2.		
3.		
4.		
5.		
Totals		

5

Values
1E $68
2E $43
3E $33
AE $19

Elvira And Chauncey Fitzbruin ... Shipmates
#227708 • Original Price: $19
Issued: 1998 • Current

1

Values	
1E	$92
2E	$72
3E	$58
AE	$35

Emma & Bailey ... Afternoon Tea
#2277 • Original Price: $18
Issued: 1996 • Retired: 1999

2

Values	
1E	$84
2E	$62
3E	$48
AE	$30

Emma ... The Witchy Bear
#2269 • Original Price: $17.50
Issued: 1995 • Retired: 1998

3

Value (U.S.)	
NE	$76

Ewell & Walton ...
Manitoba Mooselmen
(LE-12,000, Canadian Exclusive)
#BC2228 • Original Price: $24.99 (Can.)
Issued: 1996 • Retired: 1997

4

Values	
1E	$495
2E	N/A
3E	N/A
AE	N/A

Father Chrisbear And Son
#2008 • Original Price: $14.50
Issued: 1993 • Retired: 1993

5

Values	
1E	$62
2E	$44
3E	$33
AE	$20

Feldman D. Finklebearg And Dooley
..."Painless" And The Patient
#227710 • Original Price: $20
Issued: 1998 • Current

General Figurines

	Date Purchased	Price Paid	Value
1.			
2.			
3.			
4.			
5.			

Totals

49

The Bearstone Collection®

1

Values	
1E	$75
2E	$55
3E	$45
AE	$34

Flash McBear And The Sitting
#227721 • Original Price: $34
Issued: 1999 • Current

2

Values	
JAN	$96
FEB	$84
MAR	$77
APR-DEC	$66

Gary, Tina, Matt & Bailey ... From Our Home To Yours (LE-1999)
#227804 • Original Price: $48
Issued: 1999 • Retired: 1999

3

New!

Values	
1E	$16
2E	$16
3E	$16
AE	$16

Goodfer U. Bear ... Way To Go!
#227729 • Original Price: $16
Issued: 2000 • Current

4

Values	
1E	$72
2E	$58
3E	$43
AE	$19

Grace And Jonathan ... Born To Shop
#228306 • Original Price: $19
Issued: 1997 • Current

General Figurines

	Date Purchased	Price Paid	Value
1.			
2.			
3.			
4.			

Totals

1

New!

Values	
1E	$16
2E	$16
3E	$16
AE	$16

Greg McBruin ... The Wind Up
#227732 • Original Price: $16
Issued: 2000 • Current

2

Values	
1E	N/A
2E	$165
3E	$125
AE	$36
Variation	
1E	$490
2E	N/A
3E	N/A
AE	N/A

Grenville & Beatrice ... Best Friends
#2016 • Original Price: $26
Issued: 1994 • Retired: 1999
Variation: dove on right front stones

3

Values	
1E	$130
2E	$100
3E	$80
AE	$37

Grenville & Beatrice ... True Love
#2274 • Original Price: $37
Issued: 1996 • Current

4

Values	
1E	$90
2E	$66
3E	$58
AE	$32

Grenville & Knute ...
Football Buddies
#2255 • Original Price: $20
Issued: 1995 • Retired: 1998

5

Value	
NE	$35
Variation	
NE	$160

BOYDS BEARS & FRIENDS™
"Bears & Hares
you can Trust."

Grenville & Neville ... The Sign
#2099 • Original Price: $16
Issued: 1993 • Retired: 1998
Variation: brown bottom

General Figurines

	Date Purchased	Price Paid	Value
1.			
2.			
3.			
4.			
5.			

Totals

1

Values	
1E	$142
2E	$96
3E	$86
AE	$65

Grenville ... The Graduate
#2233 • Original Price: $16.50
Issued: 1994 • Retired: 1996

2

Values	
1E	$585
2E	$380
3E	$335
AE	$210

Grenville The Santabear
#2030 • Original Price: $14.50
Issued: 1994 • Retired: 1996

3

Values	
JAN	$165
FEB	$105
MAR	$89
APR-DEC	$73

Grenville ... The Storyteller
(LE-1995)
#2265 • Original Price: $47
Issued: 1995 • Retired: 1995

4

Values	
1E	$650
2E	$510
3E	N/A
AE	N/A

Grenville ... With Green Scarf
#2003-04 • Original Price: $11
Issued: 1993 • Retired: 1993

General Figurines

	Date Purchased	Price Paid	Value
1.			
2.			
3.			
4.			
5.			
		Totals	

5

Values	
1E	$96
2E	$72
3E	$62
AE	$36

Grenville With Matthew & Bailey ... Sunday Afternoon
#2281 • Original Price: $36
Issued: 1996 • Current

1

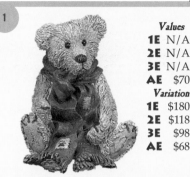

Values	
1E	N/A
2E	N/A
3E	N/A
AE	$70
Variation	
1E	$180
2E	$118
3E	$98
AE	$68

Grenville... With Red Scarf (RS)
#2003-08 • Original Price: $11
Issued: 1993 • Retired: 1995
Variation: original version

2

Values	
1E	$58
2E	$44
3E	$35
AE	$15

Guinevere The Angel... Love Is The Master Key
#228308 • Original Price: $15
Issued: 1998 • Current

3

Values	
PR	$84

Gwain & Guinevere
(QVC Premier Edition, set/2)
#99568V • Original Price: N/A
Issued: 1997 • Retired: 1997

4

Values	
1E	$43
2E	$30
3E	$15
AE	$15

Gwain... Love Is The Master Key
#228317 • Original Price: $15
Issued: 1999 • Current

5

Values	
1E	$39
2E	$27
3E	$18.50
AE	$18.50

Happy Birthday You Old Bear
(GCC Early Release)
#228321GCC • Original Price: $18.50
Issued: 1999 • Current

General Figurines

	Date Purchased	Price Paid	Value
1.			
2.			
3.			
4.			
5.			
		Totals	

The Bearstone Collection

1

Values	
1E	$125
2E	$70
3E	$55
AE	$35

Homer ... On The Plate
#2225 • Original Price: $16
Issued: 1994 • Retired: 1999

2

Values (U.S.)	
1E	$103
2E	$79
3E	$56
AE	$18

Homer On The Plate
(Canadian Exclusive)
#BC2210 • Original Price: $24.99 (Can.)
Issued: 1994 • Current

3

Value	
NE	$42

Honey B. Elfberg With Gabriella
(LE-40,000, Parade Of Gifts Exclusive)
#94577POG • Original Price: $18.50
Issued: 1998 • Retired: 1998

4

Values	
1E	$84
2E	$60
3E	$48
AE	$14

Hop-A-Long ... The Deputy
#2247 • Original Price: $14
Issued: 1995 • Current

General Figurines

	Date Purchased	Price Paid	Value
1.			
2.			
3.			
4.			

Totals

1

New!

	Values
1E	$23
2E	$23
3E	$23
AE	$23

Huck With Mandy, Zoe and Zack ... Rollin' Along
#227727 • Original Price: $23
Issued: 2000 • Current

2

	Values
1E	$48
2E	$35
3E	$30
AE	$12
	Variation
1E	$72
2E	$53
3E	$42
AE	$32

Humboldt ... The Simple Bear (RS)
#227703 • Original Price: $12
Issued: 1997 • Current
Variation: original version

3

New!

	Values
1E	$18
2E	$18
3E	$18
AE	$18

Ima Chillin ... Takin' It Easy
#227728 • Original Price: $18
Issued: 2000 • Current

4

New!

	Values
JAN	$26
FEB	$26
MAR	$26
APR-DEC	$26

Jonathan C. Tootsenwhistle With Marjorie Marchalong ... One Bear Band (LE-2000)
#227806 • Original Price: $26
Issued: 2000 • To Be Retired: 2000

5

	Values
1E	$50
2E	$37
3E	$32
AE	$27
	Variation
1E	$70
2E	$54
3E	$45
AE	$33

Judge Griz ... Hissonah (RS)
#228303 • Original Price: $18.50
Issued: 1997 • Retired: 1998
Variation: original version

General Figurines

	Date Purchased	Price Paid	Value
1.			
2.			
3.			
4.			
5.			

Totals

The Bearstone Collection®

1

Values	
1E	$150
2E	$99
3E	$80
AE	$65

Juliette Angel Bear
#2029-10 • Original Price: $13
Issued: 1994 • Retired: 1995

2

Values	
1E	$149
2E	$107
3E	$92
AE	$72

Justina & M. Harrison ... Sweetie Pies
#2015 • Original Price: $26
Issued: 1994 • Retired: 1999

3

Values	
NE	$35

Justina ... The Choir Singer
(Parade Of Gifts Exclusive)
#228324SYN • Original Price: $18
Issued: 1999 • Current

4

Values	
1E	$70
2E	$50
3E	$40
AE	$16

Justina ... The Message "Bearer"
(with two reversible signs)
#2273 • Original Price: $16
Issued: 1996 • Current

General Figurines

	Date Purchased	Price Paid	Value
1.			
2.			
3.			
4.			
5.			

Totals

5

Values	
1E	$105
2E	$85
3E	$72
AE	$54

Knute & The Gridiron
#2245 • Original Price: $16.50
Issued: 1994 • Retired: 1997

Value Guide — Boyds Bears & Friends™

1

Values	
1E	$125
2E	$88
3E	$75
AE	$49

Kringle & Bailey With List
#2235 • Original Price: $14.50
Issued: 1994 • Retired: 1999

2

Values	
1E	$89
2E	$67
3E	$53
AE	$28

Kringle And Company
#2283 • Original Price: $18
Issued: 1996 • Retired: 1999

3

Values	
1E	$125
2E	$82
3E	$70
AE	$52

Kringle And Company
(GCC Exclusive)
#2283-01 • Original Price: $18
Issued: 1996 • Retired: 1996

4

Values	
1E	$104
2E	$60
3E	$52
AE	$15

Lefty ... On The Mound
#2253 • Original Price: $15
Issued: 1995 • Current

5

Values (U.S.)	
1E	$100
2E	$70
3E	$53
AE	$30

Lefty On The Mound
(Canadian Exclusive)
#BC2066 • Original Price: $24.99 (Can.)
Issued: 1994 • Retired: 1997

General Figurines

	Date Purchased	Price Paid	Value
1.			
2.			
3.			
4.			
5.			

Totals

The Bearstone Collection®

1

Values	
1E	$45
2E	$34
3E	$28
AE	$19
Variation	
1E	$73
2E	$58
3E	$45
AE	$38

Louella & Hedda ... The Secret (RS)
#227705 • Original Price: $19
Issued: 1997 • Current
Variation: original version

2

Values (U.S.)	
1E	$215
2E	$150
3E	$95
AE	$76

Lucy Big Pig, Little Pig
(Canadian Exclusive)
#BC2050 • Original Price: $24.99 (Can.)
Issued: 1994 • Retired: 1996

3

Values	
1E	$72
2E	$57
3E	$40
AE	$24

M. Harrison's Birthday
#2275 • Original Price: $17
Issued: 1996 • Retired: 1999

4

Values	
1E	$110
2E	$82
3E	$65
AE	$26

Manheim ... The Eco-Moose
#2243 • Original Price: $15.50
Issued: 1994 • Retired: 1999

General Figurines

	Date Purchased	Price Paid	Value
1.			
2.			
3.			
4.			
5.			

Totals

5

Values	
PR	$80
1E	$55
2E	$46
3E	$36
AE	$18

Margot ... The Ballerina
#227709 • Original Price: $18
Issued: 1998 • Current

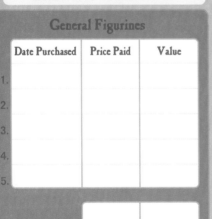

1

Values	
1E	$120
2E	$92
3E	$75
AE	$53

Maynard The Santa Moose
#2238 • Original Price: $15.50
Issued: 1994 • Retired: 1997

2

New!

Values	
1E	$19
2E	$19
3E	$19
AE	$19

Momma & Poppa McNewbear With Baby Bundles
#227731 • Original Price: $19
Issued: 2000 • Current

3

Values	
1E	$70
2E	$50
3E	$36
AE	$15

Momma McBear And Caledonia … Quiet Time
#227711 • Original Price: $15
Issued: 1998 • Current

4

Values	
1E	$82
2E	$50
3E	$38
AE	$15

Momma McBear … Anticipation
#2282 • Original Price: $15
Issued: 1996 • Current

5

Values	
1E	N/A
2E	N/A
3E	N/A
AE	$95
Variation	
1E	$235
2E	$160
3E	$125
AE	$118

Moriarty – The Bear In The Cat Suit
#2005 • Original Price: $14
Issued: 1993 • Retired: 1995
Variation: "1993" on side of base

General Figurines

	Date Purchased	Price Paid	Value
1.			
2.			
3.			
4.			
5.			

Totals

59

Value Guide — Boyds Bears & Friends™

1

Values	
1E	$35
2E	$15
3E	$15
AE	$15

Mrs. Tuttle...
Stop & Smell The Roses
#228315 • Original Price: $15
Issued: 1999 • Current

2

Values	
1E	$175
2E	$104
3E	$82
AE	$37

Ms. Bruin & Bailey ... The Lesson
#2259 • Original Price: $18.50
Issued: 1995 • Retired: 1999

3

Values	
1E	$48
2E	$35
3E	$17
AE	$17

Ms. Friday ... Take This Job ...
#228318 • Original Price: $17
Issued: 1999 • Current

4

Values	
1E	$105
2E	$75
3E	$58
AE	$38
Variation	
1E	$129
2E	$99
3E	$80
AE	$67

Ms. Griz ... Monday Morning
#2276 • Original Price: $35
Issued: 1996 • Retired: 1999
Variation: pink dress

General Figurines

	Date Purchased	Price Paid	Value
1.			
2.			
3.			
4.			
5.			

Totals

5

Values	
1E	$68
2E	$48
3E	$35
AE	$15
Variation	
1E	$88
2E	$60
3E	$46
AE	$36

Ms. Griz ... Saturday Night
#2284 • Original Price: $15
Issued: 1997 • Current
Variation: 1996 GCC Early Release

1

Value	
NE	$35

Nana Bearhugs With Austin And Haley ... Nap Time
(QVC Exclusive)
#227725V • Original Price: $16.50
Issued: 1999 • Retired: 1999

2

Values	
1E	$48
2E	$32
3E	$25
AE	$16.50
Variation	
1E	$65
2E	$42
3E	$34
AE	$25

Neville ... Compubear (RS)
#227702 • Original Price: $16.50
Issued: 1997 • Current
Variation: original version

3

Values	
1E	$145
2E	$104
3E	$83
AE	$62

Neville ... The Bedtime Bear
#2002 • Original Price: $14.50
Issued: 1993 • Retired: 1996

4

Values	
JAN	$190
FEB	$135
MAR	$118
APR-DEC	$102

Noah & Co ... Ark Builders
(LE-1996)
#2278 • Original Price: $63
Issued: 1996 • Retired: 1996

5

New!

Values	
1E	$20.50
2E	$20.50
3E	$20.50
AE	$20.50

Ol' Mother McBear ...
The More The Merrier
Classic Beary Tales
#227733 • Original Price: $20.50
Issued: 2000 • Current

General Figurines

	Date Purchased	Price Paid	Value
1.			
2.			
3.			
4.			
5.			

Totals

The Bearstone Collection

1

Values	
1E	$100
2E	$80
3E	$70
AE	$60

Otis ... Tax Time
#2262 • Original Price: $19
Issued: 1995 • Retired: 1997

2

Values	
1E	$92
2E	$66
3E	$55
AE	$36

Otis ... The Fisherman
#2249-06 • Original Price: $16
Issued: 1995 • Retired: 1998

3

Value	
NE	$60

Prince Hamalot
(LE-1997, Special Event Piece)
#01997-71 • Original Price: $30
Issued: 1997 • Retired: 1997

4

Values	
NE	$45

Prissy LaVogue ... Slave To Fashion
(GCC Exclusive)
#228322GCC • Original Price: $16.50
Issued: 1999 • Retired: 1999

General Figurines

	Date Purchased	Price Paid	Value
1.			
2.			
3.			
4.			
5.			
Totals			

5

Values	
1E	$60
2E	$45
3E	$36
AE	$18.50

Puck ... Slapshot
#228305 • Original Price: $18.50
Issued: 1997 • Current

1

Values	
1E	$65
2E	$50
3E	$37
AE	$19

Rocky Bruin … Score, Score, Score
#228307 • Original Price: $19
Issued: 1998 • Current

2

Values	
1E	$45
2E	$29
3E	$14
AE	$14

Rosemary Bearhugs … T.L.C.
#228316 • Original Price: $14
Issued: 1999 • Current

3

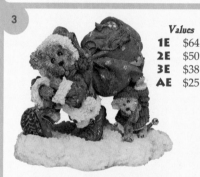

Values	
1E	$64
2E	$50
3E	$38
AE	$25

S.C. Northstar & Emmett … Lil' Helper
#228310 • Original Price: $25
Issued: 1998 • Current

4

Value	
NE	$35

S. Kringlebeary … Have A Simple Christmas
(QVC Exclusive)
#228320V • Original Price: $15
Issued: 1999 • Retired: 1999

5

Values	
1E	$129
2E	$92
3E	$72
AE	$60

Sebastian's Prayer
#2227 • Original Price: $16.50
Issued: 1994 • Retired: 1996

General Figurines

	Date Purchased	Price Paid	Value
1.			
2.			
3.			
4.			
5.			
Totals			

The Bearstone Collection

1

Values	
1E	$190
2E	$128
3E	$97
AE	$73

Sherlock & Watson...In Disguise
#2019 • Original Price: $16
Issued: 1994 • Retired: 1996

2

Values	
1E	$85
2E	$63
3E	$49
AE	$38

Simone & Bailey ... Helping Hands
#2267 • Original Price: $26
Issued: 1995 • Retired: 1999

3

Values	
1E	N/A
2E	N/A
3E	N/A
AE	$160
Variation	
1E	$420
2E	$245
3E	$180
AE	$140

Simone de Bearvoire & Her Mom,
My Auntie Alice
#2001 • Original Price: $14.50
Issued: 1993 • Retired: 1996
Variation: no patches on paws

4

Values	
1E	$98
2E	$70
3E	$53
AE	$30

Sir Edmund ... Persistence
#2279 • Original Price: $21
Issued: 1996 • Retired: 1999

General Figurines

	Date Purchased	Price Paid	Value
1.			
2.			
3.			
4.			

Totals

1

Values	
1E	$45
2E	$29
3E	$21
AE	$21

Sissie & Squirt...
Big Helper, Lil' Sipper
#228323 • Original Price: $21
Issued: 1999 • Current

2

Values	
PR	$55
1E	$50
2E	$32
3E	$26
AE	$20

Sparky & The Box
#227716 • Original Price: $20
Issued: 1999 • Current

3

Values	
1E	$68
2E	$50
3E	$38
AE	$23

Stonewall... The Rebel
#228302 • Original Price: $19
Issued: 1997 • Retired: 1999

4

Values	
JAN	$108
FEB	$88
MAR	$82
APR-DEC	$77

T.H.B. & Co...Work Is
Love Made Visible (LE-1998)
#227803 • Original Price: $63
Issued: 1998 • Retired: 1998

5

Value	
NE	$92

Tabitha With Wolsey & Zip...
Flying High
#228319 • Original Price: $26
Issued: 1999 • Retired: 1999

General Figurines		
Date Purchased	Price Paid	Value
1.		
2.		
3.		
4.		
5.		
Totals		

Value Guide — Boyds Bears & Friends™

1

Values	
1E	$180
2E	$128
3E	$93
AE	$60

Ted & Teddy
#2223 • Original Price: $16
Issued: 1994 • Retired: 1997

2

Values	
1E	$40
2E	$32
3E	$25
AE	$19

Tessa, Ben & Cissie... A Sign Of The Times
#2299 • Original Price: $19
Issued: 1999 • Current

3

New!

Values	
1E	$15
2E	$15
3E	$15
AE	$15

Tillie Hopgood... The Eggsitter
#227734 • Original Price: $15
Issued: 2000 • Current

4

New!

Values	
1E	$16
2E	$16
3E	$16
AE	$16

Tweedle Bedeedle... Stop & Smell The Flowers
#227730 • Original Price: $16
Issued: 2000 • Current

General Figurines

	Date Purchased	Price Paid	Value
1.			
2.			
3.			
4.			
5.			

Totals

5

Value	
NE	N/E

Uncle Gus & Gary... The Gift
(QVC Exclusive, set/3 with "Uncle Gus" & "Honey Bunch" *Mohair Bears*)
#99526V • Original Price: $106
Issued: 1997 • Retired: 1997

Value Guide — Boyds Bears & Friends™

1

Values	
1E	$97
2E	$70
3E	$53
AE	$42

Union Jack ... Love Letters
#2263 • Original Price: $19
Issued: 1995 • Retired: 1998

2

Value	
NE	$45

Victoria Regina Buzzbruin ...
So Many Flowers, So Little Time
(LE-1999, Special Event Piece)
#01999-71 • Original Price: $26
Issued: 1999 • Retired: 1999

3

Values	
1E	$310
2E	$230
3E	$165
AE	$68

Victoria ... The Lady
#2004 • Original Price: $18.50
Issued: 1993 • Retired: 1999

4

Values	
1E	$42
2E	$30
3E	$24
AE	$18

Wanda & Gert ...
A Little Off The Top
#227719 • Original Price: $18
Issued: 1999 • Current

5

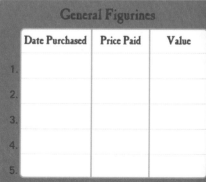

Values	
1E	$165
2E	$115
3E	$97
AE	$62

Wilson At The Beach
#2020-06 • Original Price: $16
Issued: 1994 • Retired: 1997

General Figurines

	Date Purchased	Price Paid	Value
1.			
2.			
3.			
4.			
5.			
		Totals	

Value Guide — Boyds Bears & Friends™

1

Values	
1E	$132
2E	$100
3E	$72
AE	$47

Wilson The Perfesser
#2222 • Original Price: $16.50
Issued: 1994 • Retired: 1997

2

Values	
1E	$89
2E	$63
3E	$50
AE	$35

Wilson ... The Wonderful Wizard Of Wuz
#2261 • Original Price: $16.50
Issued: 1995 • Retired: 1999

3

Values	
1E	$625
2E	$470
3E	$345
AE	$100

Wilson With Love Sonnets
#2007 • Original Price: $13
Issued: 1993 • Retired: 1997

4

Value	
NE	$55

Zoe ... The Angel Of Life
(GCC Exclusive)
#2286 • Original Price: $14
Issued: 1997 • Retired: 1997

General Figurines

	Date Purchased	Price Paid	Value
1.			
2.			
3.			
4.			
	Totals		

Holiday Pageant Series

After four years, this play's run has finally come to an end. At midnight on Dec. 31, 1999, Boyds broke the molds in the series and retired all 16 Holiday Pageant pieces.

Values	
1E	$55
2E	$38
3E	$28
AE	$18

**Ariel & Clarence...
As The Pair O' Angels**
#2411 • Original Price: $15
Issued: 1997 • Retired: 1999

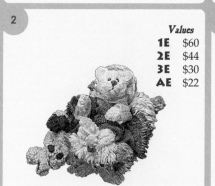

Values	
1E	$60
2E	$44
3E	$30
AE	$22

Baldwin... As The Child
#2403 • Original Price: $15
Issued: 1995 • Retired: 1999

Values	
1E	$49
2E	$38
3E	$27
AE	$22

Bruce... As The Shepherd
#2410 • Original Price: $15
Issued: 1997 • Retired: 1999

Values	
1E	$45
2E	$33
3E	$26
AE	$19

Caledonia... As The Narrator
#2412 • Original Price: $16
Issued: 1998 • Retired: 1999

Holiday Pageant Series

	Date Purchased	Price Paid	Value
1.			
2.			
3.			
4.			
		Totals	

Value Guide — Boyds Bears & Friends™

1

Values	
1E	$52
2E	$35
3E	$28
AE	$22

Essex ... As The Donkey
#2408 • Original Price: $15
Issued: 1997 • Retired: 1999

2

Values	
1E	$58
2E	$44
3E	$30
AE	$22

Heath ... As Caspar Bearing Frankincense
#2405 • Original Price: $15
Issued: 1996 • Retired: 1999

3

Values	
1E	$52
2E	$43
3E	$33
AE	$25

Matthew ... As The Drummer
#2415 • Original Price: $16
Issued: 1998 • Retired: 1999

4

Values	
1E	$52
2E	$40
3E	$33
AE	$25

Ms. Bruin ... As The Teacher
#2414 • Original Price: $16
Issued: 1998 • Retired: 1999

5

Values	
1E	$60
2E	$40
3E	$29
AE	$23

Neville ... As Joseph
#2401 • Original Price: $15
Issued: 1995 • Retired: 1999

Holiday Pageant Series

Date Purchased	Price Paid	Value
1.		
2.		
3.		
4.		
5.		

Totals

1

Values	
1E	$59
2E	$44
3E	$32
AE	$22

Raleigh … As Balthasar Bearing Myrrh
#2406 • Original Price: $15
Issued: 1996 • Retired: 1999

2

Values	
1E	$50
2E	$39
3E	$32
AE	$25

Serendipity … As The Guardian Angel
#2416 • Original Price: $16
Issued: 1998 • Retired: 1999

3

Values	
1E	$100
2E	$80
3E	$63
AE	$47

The Stage … School Pageant
#2425 • Original Price: $35
Issued: 1995 • Retired: 1999

4

Values	
1E	$62
2E	$42
3E	$29
AE	$21

Thatcher & Eden … As The Camel
#2407 • Original Price: $18
Issued: 1996 • Retired: 1999

5

Values	
1E	$64
2E	$47
3E	$30
AE	$23

Theresa … As Mary
#2402 • Original Price: $15
Issued: 1995 • Retired: 1999

Holiday Pageant Series

	Date Purchased	Price Paid	Value
1.			
2.			
3.			
4.			
5.			

Totals

The Bearstone Collection®

1

Values
1E $58
2E $44
3E $30
AE $23

Wilson...As Melchior Bearing Gold
#2404 • Original Price: $15
Issued: 1996 • Retired: 1999

2

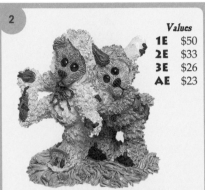

Values
1E $50
2E $33
3E $26
AE $23

Winkie & Dink...As The Lambs
#2409 • Original Price: $12
Issued: 1997 • Retired: 1999

Holiday Pageant Series

	Date Purchased	Price Paid	Value
1.			
2.			
		Totals	

Noah's Pageant Series

Three new animal pairs (and Willie as Noah's son) joined Noah's Pageant for Spring 2000, bringing the number of pieces in this series to eight. Boyds plans to release four new figurines in this series each year until 2002, when the final curtain will fall.

1

Values	
1E	$38
2E	$25
3E	$11
AE	$11

**Bernice As Mrs. Noah...
Chief Cook & Bottlewasher**
#2427 • Original Price: $11
Issued: 1999 • Current

2 New!

Values	
1E	$12
2E	$12
3E	$12
AE	$12

**Hsing Hsing And Ling Ling
Wongbruin...Carryout**
#2433 • Original Price: $12
Issued: 2000 • Current

3

Values	
1E	$38
2E	$25
3E	$11
AE	$11

Jeremy As Noah...The Ark Builder
#2426 • Original Price: $11
Issued: 1999 • Current

4 New!

Values	
1E	$12
2E	$12
3E	$12
AE	$12

**Joey And Alice Outback...
The Trekkers**
#2432 • Original Price: $12
Issued: 2000 • Current

Noah's Pageant Series

	Date Purchased	Price Paid	Value
1.			
2.			
3.			
4.			
	Totals		

1 New!

Values	
1E	$12
2E	$12
3E	$12
AE	$12

Packy And Dermah Trunkspace... Packin' Lite
#2431 • Original Price: $12
Issued: 2000 • Current

2

Values	
1E	$70
2E	$56
3E	$45
AE	$36

S. S. Noah ... The Ark
#2450 • Original Price: $36
Issued: 1999 • Current

3

Values	
1E	$27
2E	$20
3E	$11
AE	$11

Stretch & Skye Longnecker... The Lookouts
#2428 • Original Price: $11
Issued: 1999 • Current

4 New!

Values	
1E	$11
2E	$11
3E	$11
AE	$11

Willie As Noah's Son ... Tough Job But ... Somebody's Got To Do It!
#2430 • Original Price: $11
Issued: 2000 • Current

Noah's Pageant Series

	Date Purchased	Price Paid	Value
1.			
2.			
3.			
4.			
		Totals	

Other Bearstone Collectibles

You name it, Boyds has it! The company's extensive collection of Bearstone clocks, frames, musicals, ornaments, water-globes, votive holders and more is sure to appeal to any discriminating collector.

Values	
1E	$90
2E	$75
3E	$48
AE	$40

Bailey ... On Time
#27600 • Original Price: $37
Issued: 1997 • Retired: 1999

New!

Values	
1E	$19
2E	$19
3E	$19
AE	$19

Alexandra And Belle ... Telephone Tied
#27355 • Original Price: $19
Issued: 2000 • Current

Values	
1E	$44
2E	$24
3E	$24
AE	$24

Bailey ... Life Is A Daring Adventure
#27354 • Original Price: $24
Issued: 1999 • Current

Values	
1E	$53
2E	$39
3E	$33
AE	$28

Bailey ... "True Love"
#27351 • Original Price: $24
Issued: 1998 • Retired: 1999

Clocks

Date Purchased	Price Paid	Value
1.		

Frames

2.		
3.		
4.		

Totals

1

Values	
PR	$72
1E	$62
2E	$40
3E	$33
AE	$24
Variation	
NE	$52

The Collector
#27301 • Original Price: $24
Issued: 1998 • To Be Retired: 2000
Variation: 1997 GCC Early Release
"The Masterpiece"

2

Values	
PR	$72
1E	$67
2E	$35
3E	$33
AE	$28

Edmund...
The Night Before Christmas
#27302 • Original Price: $24
Issued: 1998 • Retired: 1999

3

Values	
1E	$44
2E	$24
3E	$24
AE	$24

Gary, Tina, Matt & Bailey...
A Family Portrait
#27303 • Original Price: $24
Issued: 1999 • Current

4

Values	
1E	$40
2E	$24
3E	$24
AE	$24

Rocky... All Star
#27353 • Original Price: $24
Issued: 1999 • Current

Frames

	Date Purchased	Price Paid	Value
1.			
2.			
3.			
4.			
5.			

Totals

5

Values	
1E	$56
2E	$37
3E	$32
AE	$27

Wilson... Life Is But A Dream
#27350 • Original Price: $23
Issued: 1998 • Retired: 1999

1

Values	
JAN	$58
FEB	$39
MAR	$34
APR-	
DEC	$29

Wings To Soar (LE-1997)
#27300 • Original Price: $23
Issued: 1997 • Retired: 1997

2

Values	
PR	N/E
1E	$62
2E	$53
3E	$48
AE	$39

Bailey ... The Night Before Christmas
♪ *Silver Bells*
#270501 • Original Price: $39
Issued: 1998 • Current

3

Values	
1E	$50
2E	$42
3E	$36
AE	$36

Daphne And Eloise ... Women's Work
♪ *You've Got A Friend*
#270553 • Original Price: $36
Issued: 1999 • Retired: 1999

4

Values	
1E	N/E
2E	N/E
3E	N/E
AE	N/E

Elijah & Joy ... Believe
♪ *Silver Bells*
#270503 • Original Price: $36
Issued: 1999 • Current

5

Values	
JAN	$120
FEB	$106
MAR	$96
APR-	
DEC	$89

The Flying Lesson ... This End Up (LE-1997)
#227801 • Original Price: $63
Issued: 1997 • Retired: 1997

Frames

	Date Purchased	Price Paid	Value
1.			

Musicals

2.			
3.			
4.			
5.			

Totals

The Bearstone Collection®

1

New!

Values	
1E	$38
2E	$38
3E	$38
AE	$38

Momma & Poppa McNewbear With Baby Bundles
♪ *Yes Sir That's My Baby*
#270556 • Original Price: $38
Issued: 2000 • Current

2

Values	
1E	$60
2E	$39
3E	$39
AE	$39

Ms. Bruin & Bailey ... The Lesson
♪ *I'd Like To Teach The World To Sing*
#270554 • Original Price: $39
Issued: 1999 • To Be Retired: 2000

3

New!

PHOTO UNAVAILABLE

Values	
1E	$38
2E	$38
3E	$38
AE	$38

Rosemarie And Emmie ... T.L.C.
♪ *A Spoonful Of Sugar*
#2777 • Original Price: $38
Issued: 2000 • Current

4

Values	
1E	N/E
2E	N/E
3E	N/E
AE	N/E

George And Grace ... Happily Ever After (GCC Early Release)
#27605GCC • Original Price: $45
Issued: 1999 • Current

5

Values	
1E	$27
2E	$10
3E	$10
AE	$10

Above The Clouds (ornament stand)
#25990 • Original Price: $10
Issued: 1997 • Current

Musicals		
Date Purchased	Price Paid	Value
1.		
2.		
3.		
Night Light		
4.		
Ornaments		
5.		
Totals		

Value Guide — Boyds Bears & Friends™

1

Value
NE $27

Baby's Christmas "1998" (LE-1998)
#25954 • Original Price: $13
Issued: 1998 • Retired: 1998

2

Value
NE $33

Baby's First Christmas
(NALED Exclusive)
#25703 • Original Price: $12
Issued: 1997 • Retired: 1997

3

Values
1E $27
2E $13
3E $13
AE $13

Bailey ... Home Sweet Home
#25708 • Original Price: $11
Issued: 1998 • Retired: 1999

4

Value
NE $18

Bailey ... Silver Blades
(GCC Exclusive)
#25721GCC • Original Price: $11
Issued: 1999 • Retired: 1999

5

Value
NE $23

Celestina ... Peace Angel
#25710 • Original Price: $10
Issued: 1998 • Retired: 1999

Ornaments

	Date Purchased	Price Paid	Value
1.			
2.			
3.			
4.			
5.			

Totals

1

Values
NE $25

Chandler, Constance, And Felicity ... A Brighter World (LE-1999)
#25723 • Original Price: $21
Issued: 1999 • Retired: 1999

2

Value
NE $42

Charity ... Angel Bear With Star
#2502 • Original Price: $10
Issued: 1994 • Retired: 1996

3

Values	
1E	$33
2E	$27
3E	$23
AE	$19

Clair With Gingerbread Man
#25701 • Original Price: $11
Issued: 1996 • Retired: 1998

4

Values	
1E	$16
2E	$10
3E	$10
AE	$10

Doc Buzzby ... Bee Healthy
#25716 • Original Price: $10
Issued: 1999 • Current

Ornaments

	Date Purchased	Price Paid	Value
1.			
2.			
3.			
4.			
5.			

Totals

5

Value
NE $32

Edmund ... "Believe"
#2505 • Original Price: $10
Issued: 1995 • Retired: 1997

Value Guide — Boyds Bears & Friends™

1

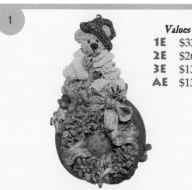

Values	
1E	$33
2E	$26
3E	$13
AE	$13

Edmund With Wreath
#25700 • Original Price: $11
Issued: 1996 • Retired: 1998

2

Value	
NE	$32

Elliot With Tree
#2507 • Original Price: $10
Issued: 1995 • Retired: 1997

3

Value	
NE	$40

Faith ... Angel Bear With Trumpet
#2500 • Original Price: $10
Issued: 1994 • Retired: 1996

4

Values	
1E	$29
2E	$20
3E	$13
AE	$13

George And Gracie ... Forever
#25707 • Original Price: $11
Issued: 1998 • Retired: 1999

5

Values	
1E	$18
2E	N/E
3E	N/E
AE	N/E

Grenville & Beatrice ...
Our Christmas (LE-1999)
#25722 • Original Price: $13
Issued: 1999 • Retired: 1999

Ornaments

	Date Purchased	Price Paid	Value
1.			
2.			
3.			
4.			
5.			

Totals

The Bearstone Collection®

1

Value
NE $40

Hope... Angel Bear With Wreath
#2501 • Original Price: $10
Issued: 1994 • Retired: 1996

2

Value
NE $18

Juliette... Love Angel
#25712 • Original Price: $10
Issued: 1998 • Retired: 1999

3

Values	
1E	$27
2E	$13
3E	$13
AE	$13

Knute... Half Time
#25705 • Original Price: $11
Issued: 1998 • Retired: 1999

4

Values	
1E	$29
2E	$14
3E	$14
AE	$14

Larry... Nuthin' But Net
#25706 • Original Price: $11
Issued: 1998 • Retired: 1999

Ornaments

	Date Purchased	Price Paid	Value
1.			
2.			
3.			
4.			
5.			
Totals			

5

Value
NE $32

Manheim The Moose With Wreath
#2506 • Original Price: $10
Issued: 1995 • Retired: 1997

Value Guide — Boyds Bears & Friends™

1

Values	
1E	$15
2E	$11
3E	$11
AE	$11

Mario... Hat Trick
#25718 • Original Price: $11
Issued: 1999 • Current

2

Value	
NE	$32

Matthew With Kip...
Baby's First Christmas "1997"
#2508 • Original Price: $10
Issued: 1997 • Retired: 1997

3

Values	
1E	$15
2E	$11
3E	$11
AE	$11

McDuffer... The 19th Hole
#25719 • Original Price: $11
Issued: 1999 • Current

4

Values	
1E	$18
2E	$11
3E	$11
AE	$11

McGwire... It's Outa Here
#25717 • Original Price: $11
Issued: 1999 • Current

5

Value	
NE	$32

McKenzie... Shootin' Star
(GCC Exclusive)
#25952GCC • Original Price: $21.50
Issued: 1998 • Retired: 1998

Ornaments

	Date Purchased	Price Paid	Value
1.			
2.			
3.			
4.			
5.			

Totals

83

Value Guide — Boyds Bears & Friends™

The Bearstone Collection®

1

Values	
1E	$20
2E	N/E
3E	N/E
AE	N/E

Nancy ... Driven To Win
(GCC Early Release)
#25720GCC • Original Price: $11
Issued: 1999 • Current

2

Value	
NE	$30

Noel Bruinski ...
Da Electrician "1998" (LE-1998)
#25953 • Original Price: $13
Issued: 1998 • Retired: 1998

3

Values	
1E	$35
2E	$13
3E	$13
AE	$13

Regina D. Ferrisdaval ...
I Am The Queen
#25709 • Original Price: $11
Issued: 1998 • Retired: 1999

4

Values	
1E	$27
2E	$13
3E	$13
AE	$13

Rocky ... Score, Score, Score
#25704 • Original Price: $11
Issued: 1998 • Retired: 1999

Ornaments

	Date Purchased	Price Paid	Value
1.			
2.			
3.			
4.			
5.			

Totals

5

Values	
1E	$16
2E	$10
3E	$10
AE	$10

Sage Buzzby ... Bee Wise
#25715 • Original Price: $10
Issued: 1999 • Current

The Bearstone Collection®

1

Value
NE $22

Serena … Joy Angel
#25711 • Original Price: $10
Issued: 1998 • Retired: 1999

2

Value
NE $35

Serendipity …
"Peace" To All (LE-1998)
#25955 • Original Price: $21
Issued: 1998 • Retired: 1998

3

Values
1E	$19
2E	$10
3E	$10
AE	$10

Sunny Buzzby … Bee Happy
#25714 • Original Price: $10
Issued: 1999 • Current

4

Values
1E	$30
2E	$25
3E	$21
AE	$16

Wilson With Shooting Star
#25702 • Original Price: $11
Issued: 1996 • Retired: 1998

5

Value
NE $50

Zoe … Starlight Christmas
(GCC Exclusive)
#25951GCC • Original Price: $21.50
Issued: 1997 • Retired: 1997

Ornaments

	Date Purchased	Price Paid	Value
1.			
2.			
3.			
4.			
5.			

Totals

1

Value
NE $35

Angelica ... In Flight
(GCC Exclusive)
#654282GCC • Original Price: $19.50
Issued: 1998 • Retired: 1998

2

Value
NE $40

Edmund ... Deck The Halls
(LE-26,500, GCC Exclusive)
#65428GCC • Original Price: $19.50
Issued: 1997 • Retired: 1997

3

Value
NE $37

Elliot The Hero (GCC Exclusive)
#654281GCC • Original Price: $20
Issued: 1998 • Retired: 1998

4

Values	
1E	$40
2E	$23
3E	$23
AE	$21

Clarence & Raphael ...
Angels Fly High
#654291 • Original Price: $21
Issued: 1998 • Current

5

Values	
1E	$44
2E	$18
3E	$18
AE	$18

Heavenly Wall Sconce
#65429 • Original Price: $16
Issued: 1997 • Retired: 1998

Plaques

	Date Purchased	Price Paid	Value
1.			
2.			
3.			

Sconces

4.			
5.			

Totals

Value Guide — Boyds Bears & Friends™

1

Values	
1E	$53
2E	$32
3E	$29
AE	$27

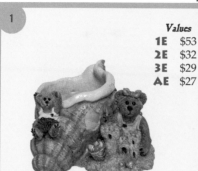

Bailey & Huck ...Wheee!!!
#27752 • Original Price: $27
Issued: 1998 • To Be Retired: 2000

2

Values	
1E	$50
2E	$29
3E	$27
AE	$27

Bailey & Matthew ... The Gift
#27723 • Original Price: $25
Issued: 1998 • Retired: 1999

3

Values	
1E	$57
2E	$36
3E	$36
AE	$28

Clarence & Angelica With Ariel ... Flight Training
#27722 • Original Price: $28
Issued: 1998 • Current

4

Values	
1E	$60
2E	$42
3E	$32
AE	$28

Daphne ... In The Cabbage Patch
#27750 • Original Price: $26
Issued: 1997 • Retired: 1999

5

Values	
1E	$73
2E	$58
3E	$45
AE	$28

Edmund The Elf Bear ... Holiday Glow
#2772 • Original Price: $26
Issued: 1996 • Retired: 1998

Votive Holders

	Date Purchased	Price Paid	Value
1.			
2.			
3.			
4.			
5.			
Totals			

1

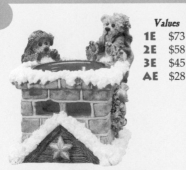

Values	
1E	$73
2E	$58
3E	$45
AE	$28

Elgin And Elliot The Elves... Toasty Warm
#2771 • Original Price: $26
Issued: 1996 • Retired: 1999

2

Values	
1E	$76
2E	$60
3E	$47
AE	$32

Emma The Witchy Bear... Pumpkin Magic
#2770 • Original Price: $26
Issued: 1996 • Retired: 1998

3

New!

Values	
1E	$14.50
2E	$14.50
3E	$14.50
AE	$14.50

Lydia... Shower Of Roses
#27755 • Original Price: $14.50
Issued: 2000 • Current

4

Values	
1E	$63
2E	$46
3E	$37
AE	$28

M. Harrison... The Ambush At Birch Tree
#27721 • Original Price: $26
Issued: 1997 • Retired: 1999

Votive Holders

	Date Purchased	Price Paid	Value
1.			
2.			
3.			
4.			

Totals

1

Values	
1E	$36
2E	$27
3E	$27
AE	$27

Marshall & Bill … Give Us Courage
#27724 • Original Price: $27
Issued: 1999 • Current

2

Values	
1E	$60
2E	$42
3E	$32
AE	$26

Maynard & Melvin… Tales Of The North
#27720 • Original Price: $26
Issued: 1997 • Retired: 1999

3

Values	
1E	$39
2E	$28
3E	$28
AE	$27
Variation	
1E	$65
2E	$44
3E	$35
AE	$29

Ms. Bruin & Bailey … Tea Time (RS)
#27751 • Original Price: $26
Issued: 1997 • To Be Retired: 2000
Variation: original version

4

Values	
1E	$50
2E	$40
3E	$27
AE	$27

Noah … And The Golden Rule
#27754 • Original Price: $27
Issued: 1999 • Current

5

Values	
1E	$56
2E	$30
3E	$30
AE	$30

Sebastian & Nicholas … The Lost Ball
#27753 • Original Price: $27
Issued: 1998 • Retired: 1999

Votive Holders

Date Purchased	Price Paid	Value
1.		
2.		
3.		
4.		
5.		

Totals

The Bearstone Collection®

1

Value
NE $73

Angelica... The Guardian
♪ *I'll Always Love You*
#2702 • Original Price: $38
Issued: 1995 • Retired: 1998

2

Values	
1E	$70
2E	$62
3E	$58
AE	$51
Variation	
1E	$85
2E	$65
3E	$60
AE	$55

The Collector
♪ *My Favorite Things*
#270551 • Original Price: $51
Issued: 1998 • Current
Variation: 1997 GCC Early Release

3

Value
NE $85

Elliot & The Tree
♪ *I'll Be Home For Christmas*
#2704 • Original Price: $36
Issued: 1995 • Retired: 1997

4

Values	
1E	$60
2E	$50
3E	$45
AE	$40

Elvira & Chauncey... Shipmates
♪ *Anchors Aweigh*
#270552 • Original Price: $38
Issued: 1999 • Retired: 1999

Waterglobes

	Date Purchased	Price Paid	Value
1.			
2.			
3.			
4.			
5.			
	Totals		

5

Value
NE $135

The Flying Lesson...
This End Up (LE-10,000)
♪ *When You Wish Upon A Star*
#270601 • Original Price: $63
Issued: 1997 • Retired: 1997

1

Values	
1E	N/E
2E	N/E
3E	N/E
AE	N/E

Grace & Jonathan ... Born To Shop
♪ *Time Of My Life*
#270502 • Original Price: $38
Issued: 1999 • Current

2

Value	
NE	$78

Grenville The Santabear
♪ *O Tannenbaum*
#2700 • Original Price: $36
Issued: 1994 • Retired: 1996

3

Values	
1E	$78
2E	$60
3E	$55
AE	$40

Homer On The Plate
♪ *Take Me Out To The Ball Game*
#270550 • Original Price: $36
Issued: 1997 • Retired: 1999

4

Value	
NE	$290

Noah & Co. (LE-1996)
♪ *Singing In The Rain*
#2706 • Original Price: $53
Issued: 1996 • Retired: 1996

5

Values	
1E	$78
2E	$55
3E	$50
AE	$45

Simone & Bailey ... Helping Hands
♪ *Skater's Waltz*
#2705 • Original Price: $36
Issued: 1996 • Retired: 1998

Waterglobes

	Date Purchased	Price Paid	Value
1.			
2.			
3.			
4.			
5.			

Totals

The Bearstone Collection®

1 New!

Values	
1E	$39
2E	$39
3E	$39
AE	$39

Tweedle Bedeedle
With Leedle And Company
♪ *Wind Beneath My Wings*
#270555 • Original Price: $39
Issued: 2000 • Current

2

Values	
1E	$50
2E	$48
3E	$48
AE	$48

Victoria Regina …
Home Sweet Hive
♪ *You Are The Sunshine Of My Life*
#270504 • Original Price: $48
Issued: 1999 • Current

3

Values	
1E	$80
2E	$63
3E	$55
AE	$47

Amelia's Enterprise
♪ *The Impossible Dream*
#2759SF • Original Price: $45
Issued: 1997 • Retired: 1999

4

Values	
1E	$113
2E	$70
3E	$57
AE	$49
Variation	
1E	$180
2E	N/A
3E	N/A
AE	N/A

Arthur On Trunk
♪ *Let Me Be Your Teddy Bear*
#2751SF • Original Price: $40
Issued: 1995 • Retired: 1997
*Variation: bear and trunk larger,
painted bottom, paw print on scarf*

Waterglobes

	Date Purchased	Price Paid	Value
1.			
2.			

San Francisco Music Boxes

3.			
4.			
5.			

Totals

5

Values	
1E	$100
2E	$77
3E	$62
AE	$48

Bailey & Emily
♪ *Teddy Bear's Picnic*
#2757SF • Original Price: $45
Issued: 1996 • Retired: 1999

1

Values	
1E	$85
2E	$62
3E	$53
AE	$45

Bailey Honey Bear
♪ *You Are The Sunshine Of My Life*
#2767SF • Original Price: $45
Issued: 1998 • Retired: 1999

2

Values	
1E	$93
2E	$77
3E	$64
AE	$43

Bailey With Suitcase
♪ *Let Me Be Your Teddy Bear*
#2755SF • Original Price: $40
Issued: 1996 • Retired: 1999

3

Values	
1E	$85
2E	$60
3E	$53
AE	$48

Bailey's Birthday
♪ *Happy Birthday*
#2763SF • Original Price: $45
Issued: 1997 • Retired: 1999

4

Values	
1E	$80
2E	$52
3E	$47
AE	$45

Born To Shop
♪ *We've Only Just Begun*
#2773SF • Original Price: $45
Issued: 1998 • Retired: 1999

5

Values	
1E	$70
2E	$55
3E	$55
AE	$55

Checkers
♪ *You Light Up My Life*
#2778SF • Original Price: $55
Issued: 1999 • Current

San Francisco Music Boxes

	Date Purchased	Price Paid	Value
1.			
2.			
3.			
4.			
5.			
Totals			

The Bearstone Collection

1

Values	
1E	$80
2E	$60
3E	$45
AE	$45

Clara The Nurse
♪ *A Spoonful Of Sugar*
#2777SF • Original Price: $45
Issued: 1999 • Retired: 1999

2

Values	
1E	$92
2E	$68
3E	$55
AE	$42

Clarence Angel
♪ *When You Wish Upon A Star*
#2753SF • Original Price: $40
Issued: 1996 • Retired: 1999

3

Values	
1E	$80
2E	$70
3E	$56
AE	$50

The Collector
♪ *My Favorite Things*
#2762SF • Original Price: $50
Issued: 1997 • Retired: 1999

4

Values	
1E	$85
2E	$65
3E	$53
AE	$47

Daphne And Eloise
♪ *You've Got A Friend*
#2760SF • Original Price: $45
Issued: 1997 • Retired: 1999

San Francisco Music Boxes

	Date Purchased	Price Paid	Value
1.			
2.			
3.			
4.			

Totals

1

Values	
1E	$40
2E	$28
3E	$23
AE	$15

Deck The Halls (ornament)
♪ *Christmas medley*
#2765SF • Original Price: $15
Issued: 1997 • Retired: 1999

2

Values	
1E	N/E
2E	N/E
3E	N/E
AE	N/E

Elliott The Hero
♪ *Gonna Fly Now*
#2780SF • Original Price: $50
Issued: 1999 • Current

3

Values	
1E	$98
2E	$75
3E	$58
AE	$47

Emma & Bailey Tea Party
♪ *Tea For Two*
#2752SF • Original Price: $45
Issued: 1996 • Retired: 1999

4

Values	
1E	$70
2E	$45
3E	$45
AE	$45

Grenville & Beatrice
♪ *Mendelssohn's "Wedding March"*
#2770SF • Original Price: $45
Issued: 1998 • Retired: 1999

5

Values	
1E	$73
2E	$45
3E	$45
AE	$45

Heart's Desire
♪ *Let Me Call You Sweetheart*
#2772SF • Original Price: $45
Issued: 1998 • Retired: 1999

San Francisco Music Boxes

	Date Purchased	Price Paid	Value
1.			
2.			
3.			
4.			
5.			

Totals

Value Guide — Boyds Bears & Friends™

1

Values	
1E	$30
2E	N/E
3E	N/E
AE	N/E

Home Sweet Home (ornament)
♪ *Home Sweet Home*
#2785SF • Original Price: $18
Issued: 1999 • Current

2

Values	
1E	$83
2E	$62
3E	$57
AE	$49

Homer On The Plate
♪ *Take Me Out To The Ball Game*
#2761SF • Original Price: $45
Issued: 1997 • Retired: 1999

3

Values	
1E	$78
2E	$50
3E	$50
AE	$50

Justina Message Bearer
♪ *I'll Have To Say
I Love You In A Song*
#2769SF • Original Price: $45
Issued: 1998 • Retired: 1999

4

Values	
1E	$85
2E	$58
3E	$53
AE	$50

Kringle & Co.
♪ *Have Yourself A Merry
Little Christmas*
#2774SF • Original Price: $50
Issued: 1998 • Retired: 1999

San Francisco Music Boxes

	Date Purchased	Price Paid	Value
1.			
2.			
3.			
4.			
5.			

Totals

5

Values	
1E	$60
2E	N/E
3E	N/E
AE	N/E

Love Is The Master Key
♪ *Can You Feel The Love Tonight*
#2779SF • Original Price: $50
Issued: 1999 • Current

Value Guide — Boyds Bears & Friends™

1

Values	
1E	$90
2E	$70
3E	$64
AE	$45

Miss Bruin & Bailey
♪ *Getting To Know You*
#2756SF • Original Price: $45
Issued: 1996 • Retired: 1999

2

Values	
1E	$89
2E	$66
3E	$57
AE	$40

Neville Bedtime
♪ *A Dream Is A Wish Your Heart Makes*
#2754SF • Original Price: $40
Issued: 1996 • Retired: 1999

3

Values	
1E	$73
2E	$50
3E	$45
AE	$45

Neville Compubear
♪ *Nine To Five*
#2768SF • Original Price: $45
Issued: 1998 • Retired: 1999

4

Values	
1E	N/E
2E	N/E
3E	N/E
AE	$18

Peace On Earth (ornament)
♪ *Twinkle, Twinkle, Little Star*
#2787SF • Original Price: $18
Issued: 1999 • Current

5

Values	
1E	N/E
2E	N/E
3E	N/E
AE	$50

Quiet Time
♪ *You Light Up My Life*
#2784SF • Original Price: $50
Issued: 1999 • Retired: 1999

San Francisco Music Boxes

	Date Purchased	Price Paid	Value
1.			
2.			
3.			
4.			
5.			

Totals

The Bearstone Collection

1

Values	
1E	$95
2E	$67
3E	$55
AE	$47

Simone & Bailey
♪ *Skater's Waltz*
#2758SF • Original Price: $45
Issued: 1996 • Retired: 1996

2

Values	
1E	$98
2E	$76
3E	$60
AE	$50
Variation	
1E	$165
2E	$150
3E	$137
AE	N/A

Ted & Teddy
♪ *For The Good Times*
#2701SF • Original Price: $45
Issued: 1995 • Retired: 1997
Variation: slightly larger bears and crate

3

Values	
1E	N/E
2E	N/E
3E	N/E
AE	$50

Telephone Tied
♪ *That's What Friends Are For*
#2782SF • Original Price: $50
Issued: 1999 • Retired: 1999

4

Values	
1E	N/E
2E	N/E
3E	N/E
AE	$18

Two Hearts, One Soul (ornament)
♪ *Love Story*
#2786SF • Original Price: $18
Issued: 1999 • Current

San Francisco Music Boxes

	Date Purchased	Price Paid	Value
1.			
2.			
3.			
4.			
5.			

Totals

5

Values	
1E	$110
2E	$85
3E	$68
AE	$57
Variation	
1E	$170
2E	$150
3E	$135
AE	N/A

Wilson With Love Sonnets
♪ *You're Nobody*
Till Somebody Loves You
#2750SF • Original Price: $40
Issued: 1995 • Retired: 1997
Variation: larger book base, sweater folds

Bearwear Pins

Boyds offers a full line of pins for collectors, including seven new pins for Spring 2000.

1

Alden & Priscilla...
The Pilgrims
Issued: 1995 • Retired
#2635 • *Value:* $10

2

Alden...Trick Or Treat
Issued: 1998 • Retired
#26022 • *Value:* $4

3

Alexandra & Belle...
Telephone Tied
Issued: 1999 • Retired
#26026 • *Value:* $4

4

Alice Spillen...Waitressing
Issued: 1999 • Retired
#26123 • *Value:* $4

5

Alice's Flight
Issued: 1995 • Retired
#2616 • *Value:* $10

6

Amelia
Issued: 1995 • Retired
#2612 • *Value:* $10

7

Angelica With Lily
Issued: 1995 • Retired
#2663 • *Value:* $12

8

Angelica's Flight
Issued: 1994 • Retired
#2605 • *Value:* $12

9

Angelique...Joy
Issued: 1999 • Retired
#26030 • *Value:* $4

10
New!

Archer...Straightshot
Issued: 2000 • Current
#26140 • *Value:* $4

11

Ariel...Love Conquers All
Issued: 1998 • Retired
#26019 • *Value:* $4

12

Arlo In The
Pumpkin Wreath
Issued: 1997 • Retired
#26012 • *Value:* $12

13

Arnold...Chip N' Putt
Issued: 1999 • Retired
#26121 • *Value:* $4

14
New!

Baby Bundles
Issued: 2000 • Current
#26139 • *Value:* $4

15

Bailey & Becky...
Diary Secrets
Issued: 1998 • Retired
#26107 • *Value:* $4

16

Bailey & Emma...
The Sisters
Issued: 1995 • Retired
#2634 • *Value:* $10

17

Bailey...Birthday Wishes
Issued: 1999 • Retired
#26117 • *Value:* $4

18

Bailey...Born To Shop
Issued: 1998 • Retired
#26016 • *Value:* $4

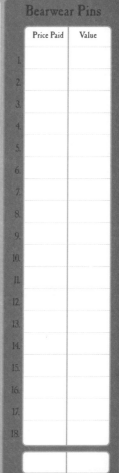

Bearwear Pins

	Price Paid	Value
1.		
2.		
3.		
4.		
5.		
6.		
7.		
8.		
9.		
10.		
11.		
12.		
13.		
14.		
15.		
16.		
17.		
18.		
Totals		

The Bearstone Collection

1

Bailey … Carpe Diem
Issued: 1999 • Retired
#26118 • *Value:* $4

2

Bailey … Chocolate Wreath
Issued: 1997 • Retired
#26104 • *Value:* $10

3

Bailey … Half Time
Issued: 1999 • Retired
#26032 • *Value:* $4

4

Bailey In Spring Bonnet
Issued: 1995 • Retired
#2667 • *Value:* $12

5

Bailey In The Garden
Issued: 1998 • Retired
#26105 • *Value:* $4

6

Bailey … Life Is
A Daring Adventure
Issued: 1998 • Retired
#26106 • *Value:* $4

7

Bailey … Love Conquers All
Issued: 1998 • Retired
#26108 • *Value:* $4

8

Bailey … Snow Angel
Issued: 1999 • Retired
#26029 • *Value:* $4

9

Bailey … Tea Time
Issued: 1997 • Retired
#26102 • *Value:* $10

10

Bailey … The Graduate
Issued: 1998 • Retired
#26109 • *Value:* $4

11

Bailey's Bonnet
Issued: 1994 • Retired
#2608 • *Value:* $16

12

Bailey's Garden
Issued: 1995 • Retired
#2615 • *Value:* $10

13

Bailey's Springtime
Issued: 1995 • Retired
#2617 • *Value:* $10

14

Bessie's Chris-moo-se
Issued: 1994 • Retired
#2604 • *Value:* $12

15

New!

Buzzby Bee Happy
Issued: 2000 • Current
#26142PO • *Value:* $6.50

16

Chandler … Light A Candle
Issued: 1999 • Retired
#26025 • *Value:* $4

17

Chrissie … Tennis Anyone?
Issued: 1999 • Retired
#26122 • *Value:* $4

18

Cryssie … Give Thanks
Issued: 1999 • Retired
#26134 • *Value:* $4

19

Clara … Get Well
Issued: 1997 • Retired
#26103 • *Value:* $4

20

Daffodil …
The Colors Of Sunshine
Issued: 1999 • Retired
#26127 • *Value:* $4

Bearwear Pins

	Price Paid	Value
1.		
2.		
3.		
4.		
5.		
6.		
7.		
8.		
9.		
10.		
11.		
12.		
13.		
14.		
15.		
16.		
17.		
18.		
19.		
20.		
Totals		

1

Dahlia...
My Biggest Blossom
Issued: 1999 • Retired
#26126 • *Value:* $4

2

Daisy...In Full Bloom
Issued: 1999 • Retired
#26130 • *Value:* $4

3

Daphne With Dove
Issued: 1995 • Retired
#2611 • *Value:* $9

4

Edmund And Bailey...
Caroling
Issued: 1996 • Retired
#26003 • *Value:* $10

5

Edmund...Deck The Halls
Issued: 1998 • Retired
#26021 • *Value:* $4

6

Edmund The Santa Bear...
Believe
Issued: 1996 • Retired
#26004 • *Value:* $10

7

Elgin The Elf Bear
Issued: 1995 • Retired
#2631 • *Value:* $10
*Variation: brown fur
trim on hat* • *Value:* N/E

8

Elliot And The Lights
Issued: 1995 • Retired
#2642 • *Value:* $10

9

Elliot Bear With
Jingle Bell Wreath
Issued: 1995 • Retired
#2636 • *Value:* $12

10

Elliot...The Fireman
Issued: 1996 • Retired
#26001 • *Value:* $9

11

Elliot With Tree
Issued: 1996 • Retired
#26002 • *Value:* $10

12

Elliot's Wreath
Issued: 1994 • Retired
#2606 • *Value:* $12

13

Emma The Witchy Bear
Issued: 1995 • Retired
#2632 • *Value:* $9

14

Ernest On
The Pumpkin Wreath
Issued: 1996 • Retired
#26005 • *Value:* $12

15

Felicity...Stocking Stuffer
Issued: 1998 • Retired
#26015 • *Value:* $4

16

Flash McBear
Issued: 1999 • Retired
#26115 • *Value:* $4

17

Grace...Born To Shop
Issued: 1997 • Retired
#26010 • *Value:* $4

18
New!
Greg McBruin...
The Windup
Issued: 2000 • Current
#26141 • *Value:* $4

19
Grenville...
The "Flakie" Santa Bear
Issued: 1997 • Retired
#26009 • *Value:* $8

20
Heather...Hugs And Kisses
Issued: 1998 • Retired
#26112 • *Value:* $4

Bearwear Pins

	Price Paid	Value
1.		
2.		
3.		
4.		
5.		
6.		
7.		
8.		
9.		
10.		
11.		
12.		
13.		
14.		
15.		
16.		
17.		
18.		
19.		
20.		
Totals		

1

Hergatroid...
Merry Christmoose
Issued: 1999 • Retired
#26027 • *Value:* $4

2

Homer
Issued: 1995 • Retired
#2618 • *Value:* $10

3
New!

Huck...Keep On Truckin'
Issued: 2000 • Current
#26138 • *Value:* $4

4
New!

Ima Chillin...Takin' It Easy
Issued: 2000 • Current
#26137 • *Value:* $4

5

Iris...Purple Passion
Issued: 1999 • Retired
#26128 • *Value:* $4

6

J.B. & The Basketballs
Issued: 1997 • Retired
#26100 • *Value:* $9

7

Juliette With Rose
Issued: 1995 • Retired
#2662 • *Value:* $12

8

Justina, Bailey & M. Harrison
Issued: 1995 • Retired
#2619 • *Value:* $10

Bearwear Pins

	Price Paid	Value
1.		
2.		
3.		
4.		
5.		
6.		
7.		
8.		
9.		
10.		
11.		
12.		
13.		
14.		
15.		
16.		
17.		
18.		
19.		
20.		
Totals		

9

Kringle & Northrop The Pup
Issued: 1997 • Retired
#26008 • *Value:* $9

10

M. Harrison
Issued: 1994 • Retired
#2601 • *Value:* $12

11

Mabel Goodheart...Practice
Random Acts Of Kindness
Issued: 1998 • Retired
#26110 • *Value:* $4

12

Margot...
Dance Dance Dance
Issued: 1998 • Retired
#26114 • *Value:* $4

13

Marigold...
Fall Is In The Air
Issued: 1999 • Retired
#26132 • *Value:* $4

14

Maxamong The Poinsettias
Issued: 1999 • Retired
#26135 • *Value:* $4

15

McKenzie...Shootin' Star
Issued: 1997 • Retired
#26006 • *Value:* $8

16

Milo...Up, Up, And Away
Issued: 1999 • Retired
#26116 • *Value:* $4

17

Mistress Bailey
Issued: 1995 • Retired
#2614 • *Value:* $12

18

Momma...Anticipation
Issued: 1999 • Retired
#26120 • *Value:* $4

19

Mrs. Tuttle
Issued: 1999 • Retired
#26024 • *Value:* $4

20

Ms. Bruin...Learn!
Issued: 1998 • Retired
#26111 • *Value:* $4

Value Guide — Boyds Bears & Friends™

1

Murgatroyd The Chrismoose
Issued: 1994 • Retired
#2603 • *Value:* **$27**

2

Nana Bear With Bailey
Issued: 1999 • Retired
#26028 • *Value:* **$4**

3

Nicholas
Issued: 1994 • Retired
#2600 • *Value:* **$12**

4

Punkin Puss
Issued: 1997 • Retired
#26014 • *Value:* **$9**

5

Punkin' Puss ... Harvest Time
Issued: 1999 • Retired
#26133 • *Value:* **$4**

6

The Queen
(Special Event Pin)
Issued: 1998 • Retired
#01998-81 • *Value:* **$12**

7

Queen Bee
(Special Event Pin)
Issued: 1999 • Retired
#01999-72 • *Value:* **$4**

8

Rocky ... Goal Kick
Issued: 1999 • Retired
#26119 • *Value:* **$4**

9

Rose ... Garden Classics
Issued: 1999 • Retired
#26129 • *Value:* **$4**

10

**S. C. Northstar ...
Ho! Ho! Ho!**
Issued: 1998 • Retired
#26017 • *Value:* **$4**

11

Sandy Claus
Issued: 1999 • Retired
#26031 • *Value:* **$4**

12

Santa Cat
Issued: 1994 • Retired
#2607 • *Value:* **$14**

13

Shelley's Flight
Issued: 1995 • Retired
#2639 • *Value:* **$10**

14

Simone In Heart Wreath
Issued: 1995 • Retired
#2679 • *Value:* **$10**

15

**Snowbeary &
The Snowflakes**
Issued: 1997 • Retired
#26007 • *Value:* **$9**

16

**Snowy ...
The First Sign Of Spring**
Issued: 1999 • Retired
#26124 • *Value:* **$4**

17

Springtime Bessie
Issued: 1995 • Retired
#2610 • *Value:* **$10**

18

PHOTO UNAVAILABLE
Stanley ... The Stick Handler
(Canadian Exclusive)
Issued: 1998 • Current
#BC94281 • *Value:* **N/E**

19

Stella ... Believe In Angels
Issued: 1998 • Retired
#26018 • *Value:* **$4**

20

Sunshine ... On My Shoulder
Issued: 1999 • Retired
#26131 • *Value:* **$4**

Bearwear Pins

	Price Paid	Value
1.		
2.		
3.		
4.		
5.		
6.		
7.		
8.		
9.		
10.		
11.		
12.		
13.		
14.		
15.		
16.		
17.		
18.		
19.		
20.		

Totals

The Bearstone Collection

1

Tulip…
An Armful Of Blooms
Issued: 1999 • Retired
#26125 • *Value:* $4

2

New!
Tweedle Bedeedle…
Stop & Smell The Flowers
Issued: 2000 • Current
#26136 • *Value:* $4

3

Wilson…Hugs & Kisses
Issued: 1997 • Retired
#26011 • *Value:* $4

4

Wilson…In Love
Issued: 1997 • Retired
#26101 • *Value:* $9

5

Wilson The Wizard…Boo!
Issued: 1998 • Retired
#26023 • *Value:* $4

6

Wilson With Love Sonnets
Issued: 1998 • Retired
#26020 • *Value:* $4

7

Wilson's Flight
Issued: 1994 • Retired
#2609 • *Value:* $15

Exclusive Pin Sets

Bearwear Pins

	Price Paid	Value
1.		
2.		
3.		
4.		
5.		
6.		
7.		

Exclusive Pin Sets

8.		
9.		
10.		
11.		

Totals

8

Amelia The Bunny, Bailey With Blue Bow & Bailey With Straw Hat (set/3)
Issued: 1996 • Retired
N/A • *Value:* N/E

9

Amelia The Bunny, Bailey With Blue Bow & Hop-A-Long (set/3)
Issued: 1995 • Retired
N/A • *Value:* N/E

10

Angelica The Angel, Bessie The Cow & Emma In Spring Bonnet (set/3)
Issued: 1996 • Retired
N/A • *Value:* N/E

11

Beatrice The Giftgiver, Clarence The Angel & Jingles The Snowman (set/3)
Issued: 1995 • Retired
N/A • *Value:* N/E

General Figurines

Boyds pencil-style figurines are interpretations of traditional folk art themes, updated with a touch of whimsy – and even a little wackiness. For Spring 2000, 12 new Folkstone pieces were introduced, including two guardian angels and a few bears and hares.

1

Values	
1E	$49
2E	$38
3E	$30
AE	$26
Variation	
1E	$70
2E	$48
3E	$35
AE	$30

Abigail … Peaceable Kingdom (GRS)
#2829 • Original Price: $19
Issued: 1995 • Retired: 1998
Variation: original version

2

Values	
1E	$63
2E	$49
3E	$38
AE	$32

Alvin T. MacBarker … Dog Face
#2872 • Original Price: $19
Issued: 1996 • Retired: 1997

3

Values	
1E	$55
2E	$44
3E	$40
AE	$33
Variation	
1E	$93
2E	$72
3E	$57
AE	$42

Angel Of Freedom (GRS)
#2820 • Original Price: $16
Issued: 1994 • Retired: 1996
Variation: original version

4

Values	
1E	$60
2E	$47
3E	$37
AE	$33
Variation	
1E	$105
2E	$75
3E	$62
AE	$45

Angel Of Love (GRS)
#2821 • Original Price: $16
Issued: 1994 • Retired: 1996
Variation: original version

General Figurines

	Date Purchased	Price Paid	Value
1.			
2.			
3.			
4.			
	Totals		

1

Values	
1E	$60
2E	$45
3E	$39
AE	$30
Variation	
1E	$93
2E	$70
3E	$50
AE	$37

Angel Of Peace (GRS)
#2822 • Original Price: $16
Issued: 1994 • Retired: 1997
Variation: original version

2

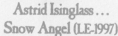

Value	
NE	$85

Astrid Isinglass...
Snow Angel (LE-1997)
#28206-06 • Original Price: $23
Issued: 1997 • Retired: 1997

3

Values	
1E	$62
2E	$42
3E	$30
AE	$19

Athena... The Wedding Angel
#28202 • Original Price: $19
Issued: 1996 • Current

4

Values	
1E	$35
2E	$23
3E	$19
AE	$19

Audubon P. Pussywillow...
The Birdwatcher
#2868 • Original Price: $19
Issued: 1999 • Current

General Figurines

	Date Purchased	Price Paid	Value
1.			
2.			
3.			
4.			
5.			

Totals

5

Values	
PR	$66
1E	$59
2E	$36
3E	$27
AE	$20

Auntie Cocoa M. Maximus...
Chocolate Angel
#28242 • Original Price: $20
Issued: 1998 • Current

1

Values	
1E	$48
2E	$34
3E	$27
AE	$23

Bearly Nick And Buddies
#28001 • Original Price: $19.50
Issued: 1997 • Retired: 1999

2

Values	
1E	$55
2E	$38
3E	$30
AE	$26
Variations 1 & 2	
1E	$65
2E	$48
3E	$35
AE	$27

Beatrice … The Birthday Angel (GRS)
#2825 • Original Price: $19
Issued: 1995 • Retired: 1998
Variation 1: hard to read writing on bow
Variation 2: taller

3

Values	
1E	$62
2E	$45
3E	$40
AE	$28

Beatrice … The Giftgiver
#2836 • Original Price: $18
Issued: 1995 • Retired: 1999

4

Values	
1E	$52
2E	$37
3E	$30
AE	$26

Bernie …
Igotwatiwanted St. Bernard Santa
#2873 • Original Price: $18
Issued: 1996 • Retired: 1999

5

Values	
1E	N/A
2E	N/A
3E	N/A
AE	$29
Variation	
1E	$87
2E	$66
3E	$50
AE	$45

Betty Biscuit
#2870 • Original Price: $19
Issued: 1996 • Retired: 1999
Variation: "Betty Cocker"

General Figurines

Date Purchased	Price Paid	Value
1.		
2.		
3.		
4.		
5.		
Totals		

The Folkstone Collection

1

Values	
1E	$50
2E	$37
3E	$29
AE	$20

Birdie Holeinone...
NQGA Of Golfers
#28245 • Original Price: $20
Issued: 1998 • Current

2

Values	
1E	$52
2E	$36
3E	$29
AE	$21
Variation	
1E	$65
2E	$50
3E	$39
AE	$30

Boowinkle Von Hindenmoose (GRS)
#2831 • Original Price: $18
Issued: 1995 • Retired: 1998
Variation: original version

3

Value	
NE	$48

Bristol... Just Sweepin'
(Catalog Exclusive)
#28101 • Original Price: $17
Issued: 1997 • Retired: 1997

4

Values	
1E	$58
2E	$42
3E	$33
AE	$26

Buster Goes a' Courtin'
#2844 • Original Price: $19
Issued: 1996 • Retired: 1998

General Figurines

Date Purchased	Price Paid	Value
1.		
2.		
3.		
4.		

Totals

1

New!

Values	
1E	$20
2E	$20
3E	$20
AE	$20

Calliope Clipsalot With Pinchy...
Guardian Angel Of Pennies
#28211 • Original Price: $20
Issued: 2000 • Current

2

Values	
1E	$34
2E	$19
3E	$19
AE	$19

Chilly & Millie...Starlights
#28106 • Original Price: $19
Issued: 1999 • Current

3

Values	
1E	$90
2E	$65
3E	$50
AE	$33

Chilly & Son With Dove
#2811 • Original Price: $16
Issued: 1994 • Retired: 1997

4

Value	
NE	$98

Constance & Felicity...
Best Friend Angels (LE-1997)
#28205 • Original Price: $38
Issued: 1997 • Retired: 1997

5

Values	
1E	$68
2E	$50
3E	$42
AE	$19

Cosmos...The Gardening Angel
#28201 • Original Price: $19
Issued: 1996 • Current

General Figurines

	Date Purchased	Price Paid	Value
1.			
2.			
3.			
4.			
5.			
Totals			

1

Values	
1E	$40
2E	$25
3E	$20
AE	$20

Domestica T. Whirlwind ...
NQGA Of Super Moms
#28249 • Original Price: $20
Issued: 1999 • Current

2

Values	
1E	$33
2E	$19
3E	$19
AE	$19

Dr. R.X. Mooselberry ...
Making Rounds
#28301 • Original Price: $19
Issued: 1999 • To Be Retired: 2000

3

Values	
1E	$60
2E	$36
3E	$27
AE	$23

Egon ... The Skier
#2837 • Original Price: $18
Issued: 1996 • Retired: 1999

4

Values	
1E	$37
2E	$19
3E	$19
AE	$19

Electronick & Splice ... The Surprise
#28004 • Original Price: $19
Issued: 1999 • Current

General Figurines

	Date Purchased	Price Paid	Value
1.			
2.			
3.			
4.			
5.			

Totals

5

Values	
1E	$60
2E	$36
3E	$26
AE	$20

Elmer ... Been Farmin' Long?
#2851 • Original Price: $18
Issued: 1995 • Retired: 1998

1

Values	
1E	$62
2E	$44
3E	$37
AE	$28

Elmo "Tex" Beefcake... On The Range
#2853 • Original Price: $19
Issued: 1996 • Retired: 1997

2

Values	
1E	$66
2E	$47
3E	$39
AE	$26

Ernest Hemmingmoose... The Hunter
#2835 • Original Price: $18
Issued: 1995 • Retired: 1999

3

Values	
1E	$65
2E	$42
3E	$32
AE	$28

Esmeralda... The Wonderful Witch
#2860 • Original Price: $18
Issued: 1995 • Retired: 1999

4

Value	
NE	$189

Etheral... Angel Of Light (LE-7,200)
#28203-06 • Original Price: $19
Issued: 1996 • Retired: 1996

5

Values	
1E	$57
2E	$37
3E	$28
AE	$24

Execunick... The First Global Business Man
#28002 • Original Price: $21
Issued: 1998 • Retired: 1999

General Figurines

	Date Purchased	Price Paid	Value
1.			
2.			
3.			
4.			
5.			

Totals

1

Values	
1E	$60
2E	$40
3E	$30
AE	$25

Flora & Amelia ... The Gardeners
#2843 • Original Price: $19
Issued: 1996 • Retired: 1999

2

Values	
1E	$60
2E	$42
3E	$33
AE	$22

Flora, Amelia & Eloise ... The Tea Party
#2846 • Original Price: $19
Issued: 1996 • Retired: 1999

3

Values	
1E	$60
2E	$52
3E	$45
AE	$40
Variations 1 & 2	
1E	$88
2E	$59
3E	$50
AE	$40

Florence ... The Kitchen Angel (GRS)
#2824 • Original Price: $19
Issued: 1995 • Retired: 1996
Variation 1: hand on bottom center of bowl
Variation 2: longer skirt

4

Values	
PR	$60
1E	$50
2E	$37
3E	$29
AE	$23

Francoise & Suzanne ... The Spree
#2875 • Original Price: $20
Issued: 1998 • To Be Retired: 2000

General Figurines

Date Purchased	Price Paid	Value
1.		
2.		
3.		
4.		

Totals

1

Values	
1E	$33
2E	$19
3E	$19
AE	$19

Fuzznick With Claws & Co.
#28003 • Original Price: $19
Issued: 1999 • Current

2

Values	
1E	$33
2E	$19
3E	$19
AE	$19

Harriet & Punch With Hermaine ... The Challenge
#28402 • Original Price: $19
Issued: 1999 • Current

3

New!

Values	
1E	$19
2E	$19
3E	$19
AE	$19

Heather With Chris ... Guardian Angel Of Volleyball
#28210 • Original Price: $19
Issued: 2000 • Current

4

Values	
1E	$50
2E	$33
3E	$28
AE	$24

Helga With Ingrid & Anna ... Be Warm
#2818 • Original Price: $19
Issued: 1997 • Retired: 1999

5

New!

Values	
1E	$20
2E	$20
3E	$20
AE	$20

Honker T. Flatfoot ... Send In The Clowns
#2887 • Original Price: $20
Issued: 2000 • Current

General Figurines

	Date Purchased	Price Paid	Value
1.			
2.			
3.			
4.			
5.			

Totals

The Folkstone Collection®

1

Values	
1E	$53
2E	$38
3E	$26
AE	$20

I.B. Coldman ... Ice Is Nice
#28102 • Original Price: $20
Issued: 1998 • To Be Retired: 2000

2

Values	
1E	$65
2E	$48
3E	$38
AE	$32

Ichabod Mooselman ... The Pilgrim
#2833 • Original Price: $18
Issued: 1995 • Retired: 1997

3

Values	
1E	$42
2E	$31
3E	$27
AE	$24
Variation	
1E	$66
2E	$42
3E	$34
AE	$24

Ida & Bessie ... The Gardeners (GRS)
#2852 • Original Price: $18
Issued: 1995 • Retired: 1998
Variation: original version

4

Value	
NE	$50

Ike & Libby ...
"Stars & Stripes Forever"
(Catalog Exclusive)
#281035SYN • Original Price: $20
Issued: 1998 • Retired: 1998

General Figurines

Date Purchased	Price Paid	Value
1.		
2.		
3.		
4.		
5.		

Totals

5

Values	
1E	$83
2E	$54
3E	$40
AE	$26

Illumina ... Angel Of Light
#28203 • Original Price: $19
Issued: 1996 • Retired: 1999

1

	Values
JAN	$40
FEB	N/E
MAR	N/E
APR-DEC	N/E

Isabella ... Follow Your Heart's Desire (LE-1999)
#28208 • Original Price: $24
Issued: 1999 • Retired: 1999

2

New!

	Values
1E	$20.50
2E	$20.50
3E	$20.50
AE	$20.50

Jack Hammer ... Hard Hat
#2885 • Original Price: $20.50
Issued: 2000 • Current

3

	Values
1E	$44
2E	$26
3E	$22
AE	$19
	Variation
1E	$60
2E	$35
3E	$27
AE	$23

Jean Claude & Jacque ... The Skiers (GRS)
#2815 • Original Price: $17
Issued: 1995 • Retired: 1999
Variation: original version

4

	Values
1E	$108
2E	$62
3E	$43
AE	$39

Jill ... Language Of Love
#2842 • Original Price: $18
Issued: 1995 • Retired: 1997

5

	Values
1E	$75
2E	$58
3E	$52
AE	$44
	Variation
1E	$123
2E	$80
3E	$69
AE	$60

Jingle Moose (GRS)
#2830 • Original Price: $16
Issued: 1994 • Retired: 1996
Variation: original version

General Figurines

Date Purchased	Price Paid	Value
1.		
2.		
3.		
4.		
5.		

Totals

The Folkstone Collection

1

Values	
1E	$110
2E	$75
3E	$62
AE	$50

Jingles & Son With Wreath
#2812 • Original Price: $16
Issued: 1994 • Retired: 1996

2

Values	
1E	$68
2E	$44
3E	$31
AE	$23

Krystal Isinglass ... Snow Angel
#28206 • Original Price: $19
Issued: 1997 • Retired: 1999

3

Values	
1E	$35
2E	$18
3E	$18
AE	$18

**Laverne B. Bowler ...
Strikes & Spares**
#28428 • Original Price: $18
Issued: 1999 • Current

4

Value	
NE	$110

**Liddy Pearl ... How Does
Your Garden Grow (LE-1998)**
#2881 • Original Price: $40
Issued: 1998 • Retired: 1998

General Figurines

	Date Purchased	Price Paid	Value
1.			
2.			
3.			
4.			
5.			
	Totals		

5

Values	
1E	$53
2E	$36
3E	$32
AE	$28
Variations 1 & 2	
1E	$70
2E	$52
3E	$42
AE	$37

Lizzie ... The Shopping Angel (GRS)
#2827 • Original Price: $19
Issued: 1995 • Retired: 1998
Variation 1: hand on strap 1/2" above purse
Variation 2: many folds in skirt

1

Values	
1E	$57
2E	$36
3E	$30
AE	$26

Loretta Moostein...
Yer Cheatin' Heart
#2854 • Original Price: $19
Issued: 1996 • Retired: 1999

2

Values	
AE	$23
Variation	
1E	$58
2E	$44
3E	$32
AE	$28

Lucky McPlug
#2871 • Original Price: $19
Issued: 1996 • Retired: 1999
Variation: "Sparky McPlug"

3

Value	
NE	$62

Luminette... By The Light
Of The Silvery Moon (LE-1998)
#28207-06 • Original Price: $24
Issued: 1998 • Retired: 1998

4

Values	
1E	$50
2E	$36
3E	$29
AE	$19

Luna... By The Light
Of The Silvery Moon
#28207 • Original Price: $19
Issued: 1998 • To Be Retired: 2000

5

Values	
1E	$53
2E	$33
3E	$28
AE	$19

Madge... The Magician/Beautician
#28243 • Original Price: $19
Issued: 1997 • Current

General Figurines		
Date Purchased	Price Paid	Value
1.		
2.		
3.		
4.		
5.		
Totals		

117

The Folkstone Collection®

1

Values	
1E	$53
2E	$37
3E	$28
AE	$19

Mercy ... Angel Of Nurses
#28240 • Original Price: $19
Issued: 1997 • Current

2

Values	
1E	$50
2E	$36
3E	$26
AE	$19

**Miliken Von Hinden Moose ...
Tree's Company**
#2832 • Original Price: $19
Issued: 1998 • Current

3

Values	
1E	$52
2E	$37
3E	$30
AE	$25
Variation	
1E	$62
2E	$48
3E	$35
AE	$29

Minerva ... The Baseball Angel
#2826 • Original Price: $19
Issued: 1995 • Retired: 1997
Variation: 6 buttons below belt

4

Values	
1E	$42
2E	$33
3E	$26
AE	$17.50

**Miss Prudence P. Carrotjuice ...
Multiplication**
#2848 • Original Price: $17.50
Issued: 1998 • Current

General Figurines

Date Purchased	Price Paid	Value
1.		
2.		
3.		
4.		
5.		

Totals

5

New!

Values	
1E	$20
2E	$20
3E	$20
AE	$20

**Momma McHutch And Babies ...
Family Matters**
#28403 • Original Price: $20
Issued: 2000 • Current

1

Values	
1E	$52
2E	$36
3E	$28
AE	$23

Montague Von Hindenmoose...
Surprise!
#2839 • Original Price: $19
Issued: 1997 • Retired: 1999

2

Values	
1E	$25
2E	$19
3E	$19
AE	$19
Variation	
1E	$50
2E	$38
3E	$30
AE	$25

Ms. Fries...
Guardian Angel Of Waitresses
#28246 • Original Price: $19
Issued: 1999 • Current
Variation: 1998 GCC Early Release
"Ms. Fries ... Not Quite The Guardian
Angel Of Waitresses"

3

Values	
1E	$45
2E	$35
3E	$28
AE	$24
Variation	
PR	$60
NE	$56

Ms. Imin Payne...
NOGA Of Exercise
#28244 • Original Price: $20
Issued: 1998 • Retired: 1999
Variation: 1998 GCC Early Release
"Iown Payne ... Aerobics Angel"

4

Values	
1E	$38
2E	$25
3E	$20
AE	$20

Ms. McFrazzle...
Daycare Extraordinaire
#2883 • Original Price: $20
Issued: 1999 • Current

5

Values	
1E	$62
2E	$40
3E	$33
AE	$28

Ms. Patience... Angel Of Teachers
#28241 • Original Price: $19
Issued: 1997 • Retired: 1998

General Figurines

Date Purchased	Price Paid	Value
1.		
2.		
3.		
4.		
5.		

Totals

The Folkstone Collection

1

	Values
1E	$35
2E	$19
3E	$19
AE	$19

Ms. Pleasant ... May I Help You?
#28250 • Original Price: $19
Issued: 1999 • Current

2

	Values
1E	$35
2E	$19
3E	$19
AE	$19

Murphy McFrost ... Fire & Ice
#28105 • Original Price: $19
Issued: 1999 • Current

3

	Values
1E	$37
2E	$21
3E	$21
AE	$21

Myron R. Fishmeister ...
Angel Of Fish Stories
#28247 • Original Price: $21
Issued: 1999 • Current

4

	Values
1E	$66
2E	$40
3E	$32
AE	$27

Myrtle ... Believe!
#2840 • Original Price: $18
Issued: 1995 • Retired: 1998

General Figurines

Date Purchased	Price Paid	Value
1.		
2.		
3.		
4.		
5.		

Totals

5

	Values
1E	$45
2E	$36
3E	$25
AE	$20

Nana McHare And
The Love Gardeners
#2849 • Original Price: $19
Issued: 1998 • Current

1

Value	
NE	$165

Na-Nick And Siegfried...
The Plan (LE-10,000)
#2807 • Original Price: $34
Issued: 1996 • Retired: 1996

2

Values	
1E	$59
2E	$40
3E	$27
AE	$22
Variation	
1E	$72
2E	$50
3E	$40
AE	$28

Na-Nick Of The North (GRS)
#2804 • Original Price: $18
Issued: 1995 • Retired: 1999
Variation: original version

3

Values	
1E	$58
2E	$35
3E	$29
AE	$25

Nanny...The Snowmom
#2817 • Original Price: $18
Issued: 1996 • Retired: 1998

4

Values	
1E	$108
2E	$65
3E	$44
AE	$35

Nicholai With Tree
#2800 • Original Price: $17
Issued: 1994 • Retired: 1997

5

Values	
1E	$108
2E	$70
3E	$53
AE	$37

Nicholas With Book Of Lists
#2802 • Original Price: $17
Issued: 1994 • Retired: 1996

General Figurines

Date Purchased	Price Paid	Value
1.		
2.		
3.		
4.		
5.		

Totals

The Folkstone Collection®

1

Values	
1E	$60
2E	$39
3E	$32
AE	$27

Nicknoah ... Santa With Ark
#2806 • Original Price: $18
Issued: 1996 • Retired: 1999

2

Values	
1E	$98
2E	$62
3E	$45
AE	$34

Niki With Candle
#2801 • Original Price: $17
Issued: 1994 • Retired: 1997

3

Values	
1E	$65
2E	$45
3E	$40
AE	$29

No-No-Nick ... Bad Boy Santa
#2805 • Original Price: $18
Issued: 1996 • Retired: 1998

4

Values	
1E	$50
2E	$38
3E	$30
AE	$24
Variation	
1E	$68
2E	$52
3E	$40
AE	$30

Northbound Willie (GRS)
#2814 • Original Price: $17
Issued: 1995 • Retired: 1997
Variation: original version

General Figurines

Date Purchased	Price Paid	Value
1.		
2.		
3.		
4.		
5.		

Totals

5

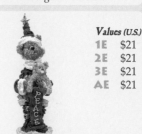

Values *(U.S.)*	
1E	$21
2E	$21
3E	$21
AE	$21

Nottaway & Hope ...
Northern Peace
(LE-15,000, Canadian Exclusive)
#BC2884PO • Original Price: $29.99 (Can.)
Issued: 1999 • Current

1

Values	
1E	$58
2E	$41
3E	$32
AE	$18
Variation	
1E	$112
2E	$68
3E	$49
AE	$38

Oceania ... Ocean Angel (GRS)
#2823 • Original Price: $16
Issued: 1995 • Retired: 1998
Variation: original version

2

Values	
1E	$57
2E	$40
3E	$32
AE	$25

Olaf ... Mogul Meister
#2819 • Original Price: $16.50
Issued: 1997 • Retired: 1998

3

Values	
1E	$48
2E	$34
3E	$28
AE	$19

P. J. McSnoozin With Craxton ... Hibearnation
#2882 • Original Price: $19
Issued: 1998 • Current

4

Values	
1E	$44
2E	$35
3E	$27
AE	$24
Variation	
1E	$48
2E	$38
3E	$30
AE	$27

Peacenik ... The Sixties Santa
#2809 • Original Price: $20
Issued: 1998 • Retired: 1999
Variation: 1997 GCC Early Release
"Peace-Nick"

5

Values	
1E	$50
2E	$49
3E	$32
AE	$27
Variation	
1E	$70
2E	$47
3E	$37
AE	$30

Peter ... The Whopper (GRS)
#2841 • Original Price: $18
Issued: 1995 • Retired: 1997
Variation: original version

General Figurines

Date Purchased	Price Paid	Value
1.		
2.		
3.		
4.		
5.		
Totals		

The Folkstone Collection

1

Values	
1E	$64
2E	$53
3E	$40
AE	$19

Polaris And The North Star...
On Ice
#2880 • Original Price: $19
Issued: 1997 • To Be Retired: 2000

2

Values	
1E	$49
2E	$37
3E	$30
AE	$19

Prudence...Daffodils
#2847 • Original Price: $19
Issued: 1997 • To Be Retired: 2000

3

Values	
1E	$65
2E	$52
3E	$42
AE	$34

Prudence Mooselmaid...
The Pilgrim
#2834 • Original Price: $18
Issued: 1995 • Retired: 1997

4

Values	
1E	$40
2E	$29
3E	$24
AE	$21

Purrscilla G. Pussenboots...
Mitten Knitters
#2865 • Original Price: $21
Issued: 1998 • Current

General Figurines

	Date Purchased	Price Paid	Value
1.			
2.			
3.			
4.			

Totals

1

Values	
1E	$52
2E	$37
3E	$32
AE	$19

Purrscilla ... Give Thanks
#2866 • Original Price: $19
Issued: 1998 • Current

2

Values	
1E	$58
2E	$40
3E	$30
AE	$25

Robin ... The Snowbird Lover
#2816 • Original Price: $18
Issued: 1996 • Retired: 1999

3

Values	
1E	$44
2E	$30
3E	$27
AE	$23
Variation	
1E	$55
2E	$37
3E	$30
AE	$25

Rufus ... Hoe Down (GRS)
#2850 • Original Price: $18
Issued: 1995 • Retired: 1999
Variation: original version

4

Values	
1E	$60
2E	$40
3E	$35
AE	$27
Variation	
1E	$63
2E	$49
3E	$36
AE	$29

St. Nick ... The Quest
#2808 • Original Price: $20
Issued: 1996 • Retired: 1996
Variation: 1996 GCC Early Release

5

Values	
PR	$52
1E	$23
2E	$19
3E	$19
AE	$19

Salem ... Give Thanks
#2867 • Original Price: $19
Issued: 1999 • Current

General Figurines

	Date Purchased	Price Paid	Value
1.			
2.			
3.			
4.			
5.			

Totals

The Folkstone Collection®

1

New!

Values	
1E	$40
2E	$40
3E	$40
AE	$40

PROUD TO SERVE

Sam, Libby And Ellis...
Fife And Drum
#2886 • Original Price: $40
Issued: 2000 • Current

2

Values	
1E	$52
2E	$42
3E	$34
AE	$26
Variation	
1E	$70
2E	$49
3E	$39
AE	$32

Seraphina With Jacob & Rachael...
The Choir Angels (GRS)
#2828 • Original Price: $20
Issued: 1995 • Retired: 1997
Variation: original version

3

Values	
1E	$64
2E	$45
3E	$34
AE	$19

Serenity... The Mother's Angel
#28204 • Original Price: $19
Issued: 1996 • Current

4

Values	
1E	$56
2E	$40
3E	$34
AE	$24

Sgt. Rex & Matt... The Runaway
#2874 • Original Price: $19.50
Issued: 1997 • Retired: 1999

General Figurines

Date Purchased	Price Paid	Value
1.		
2.		
3.		
4.		
	Totals	

1

Values	
1E	$50
2E	$38
3E	$30
AE	$23
Variation	
1E	$72
2E	$50
3E	$35
AE	$26

Siegfried & Egon ... The Sign (GRS)
#2899 • Original Price: $17
Issued: 1995 • Retired: 1998
Variation: original version

2

Values	
1E	$52
2E	$38
3E	$29
AE	$24
Variation	
1E	$68
2E	$45
3E	$38
AE	$31

Sliknick ...
The Chimney Sweep (GRS)
#2803 • Original Price: $18
Issued: 1995 • Retired: 1998
Variation: original version

3

New!

Values	
1E	$19
2E	$19
3E	$19
AE	$19

Solstice Angeldance ... Sunlight
#28209 • Original Price: $19
Issued: 2000 • Current

4

Values	
1E	$58
2E	$39
3E	$30
AE	$26

"Too Loose" Lapin ...
"The Arte-e-st"
#2845 • Original Price: $19
Issued: 1996 • Retired: 1999

5

Values	
1E	N/A
2E	$20
3E	$20
AE	$20
Variation	
1E	$36
2E	N/A
3E	N/A
AE	N/A

Wendy Willowhare ...
A Tisket A Tasket
#28401 • Original Price: $20
Issued: 1999 • Current
Variation: "Wendy Willowhare &
Pip ... A Tisket A Tasket"

General Figurines

Date Purchased	Price Paid	Value
1.		
2.		
3.		
4.		
5.		

Totals

1

Values	
1E	$115
2E	$83
3E	$68
AE	$53

Windy With Book
#2810 • Original Price: $16
Issued: 1994 • Retired: 1996

2

Values	
1E	$50
2E	$35
3E	$29
AE	$24

Ziggy ... The Duffer
#2838 • Original Price: $19
Issued: 1997 • Retired: 1999

3

Values	
AE	$19
Variation	
1E	$42
2E	$33
3E	$28
AE	$23

Zip Shovelenhand ... Got Snow?
#28104 • Original Price: $19
Issued: 1999 • Current
Variation: "Zambonie . . . Got Snow?"

General Figurines

	Date Purchased	Price Paid	Value
1.			
2.			
3.			
		Totals	

Carvers Choice

Years ago, Boyds sold hand carved wooden ornaments and duck decoys. The *Carvers Choice* resin figurines recapture that folk art style. Although 1999 saw the release of some open edition pieces, all six Spring 2000 figurines are limited editions.

Values	
1E	$16
2E	$16
3E	$16
AE	$16

Avery Frostbuns...Open House
#370109 • Original Price: $16
Issued: 1999 • Current

Values	
PR	$88
NE	$65

Barnaby...Homeward Bound
(LE-18,000)
#370001 • Original Price: $38
Issued: 1998 • Retired: 1998

Values	
1E	$34
2E	$26
3E	$23
AE	$23

Barnaby Jr...Homeward Bound
#370101 • Original Price: $19
Issued: 1998 • Retired: 1999

Values	
PR	$83
NE	$58

Burt...Bundle Up (LE-18,000)
#370002 • Original Price: $20
Issued: 1998 • Retired: 1998

Carvers Choice

	Date Purchased	Price Paid	Value
1.			
2.			
3.			
4.			
Totals			

129

Values

1E $33
2E $17
3E $17
AE $17

Burt Jr ... Bundle Up
#370102 • Original Price: $14
Issued: 1998 • Retired: 1999

Values

PR $60
NE $48

Chester Bigheart ... Love Much
(LE-12,000)
#370053 • Original Price: $27
Issued: 1999 • Retired: 1999

Values

1E $14
2E $14
3E $14
AE $14

Flipper Cleansweep ...
No Job's Too Big
#370108 • Original Price: $14
Issued: 1999 • Current

Values

1E $16
2E $16
3E $16
AE $16

I.M. Ketchikan ... Stringin' Along
#370110 • Original Price: $16
Issued: 1999 • Current

Carvers Choice

	Date Purchased	Price Paid	Value
1.			
2.			
3.			
4.			
5.			

Totals

Value
NE N/E

Iditarod With Tom, Dick & Harry ...
Winter Magic (LE-7,200)
#370009 • Original Price: $31
Issued: 1999 • Retired: 1999

The Folkstone Collection®

130

1

Values	
1E	$16
2E	$16
3E	$16
AE	$16

J.R. Fairbanks ... Freeze Enterprise
#370105 • Original Price: $16
Issued: 1999 • Current

2

Values	
PR	$59
1E	$45
2E	$34
3E	$34
AE	$34

Jester Q. Funnybones ... Laugh Often
#370054 • Original Price: $27
Issued: 1999 • Retired: 1999

3

Values	
1E	$42
2E	$35
3E	$35
AE	$35

Lady Harriet Rushmore ... Never Enough Time
#370050 • Original Price: $31
Issued: 1999 • Retired: 1999

4

New!

Value	
NE	$18

Maribel Moonbeam ... Top Of The Moon (LE-2000)
#370055 • Original Price: $18
Issued: 2000 • To Be Retired: 2000

5

New!

Value	
NE	$16

Merino Woolmore And Chauncey ... The Speedsters (LE-2000)
#370056 • Original Price: $16
Issued: 2000 • To Be Retired: 2000

Carvers Choice

	Date Purchased	Price Paid	Value
1.			
2.			
3.			
4.			
5.			
Totals			

1

Values	
1E	$17
2E	$17
3E	$17
AE	$17

Mrs. C. With Bobbin... As Good As New
#370107 • Original Price: $17
Issued: 1999 • Current

2

Value	
NE	N/E

Nicholas Tacklebox With Bobber... Frozen Fish (LE-7,200)
#370005 • Original Price: $27
Issued: 1999 • Retired: 1999

3

PHOTO UNAVAILABLE

Values	
1E	$17
2E	$17
3E	$17
AE	$17

Nick Tacklebox, Jr. With Bob... Frozen Minnows
#370106 • Original Price: $17
Issued: 1999 • Current

4

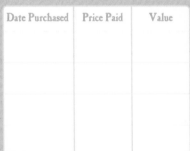

Value	
NE	N/E

Northwind Nick... Onward Bound (LE-1999)
#370008 • Original Price: $31
Issued: 1999 • Retired: 1999

Carvers Choice

	Date Purchased	Price Paid	Value
1.			
2.			
3.			
4.			
Totals			

1

New!

Value
NE $11.50

Percy Tunabreath ... Got Fish?
(LE-2000)
#370060 • Original Price: $11.50
Issued: 2000 • To Be Retired: 2000

2

Value
NE N/E

St. Nick With Parker ... Wide Load
(LE-7,200)
#370006 • Original Price: $27
Issued: 1999 • Retired: 1999

3

Values
PR $100
NE $80

Santa ... And The Final Inspection
(LE-18,000)
#370003 • Original Price: $53
Issued: 1998 • Retired: 1998

4

Values
PR $100
NE $80

Santa ... In The Nick Of Time
(LE-18,000)
#370000 • Original Price: $48
Issued: 1998 • Retired: 1998

5

Values
1E $40
2E $27
3E $27
AE $27

Santa Jr ... And The Final Inspection
#370103 • Original Price: $24
Issued: 1998 • Retired: 1999

Carvers Choice

	Date Purchased	Price Paid	Value
1.			
2.			
3.			
4.			
5.			

Totals

Values

1E	$40
2E	$26
3E	$26
AE	$26

Santa Jr ... In The Nick Of Time
#370100 • Original Price: $23
Issued: 1998 • Retired: 1999

Values

1E	$40
2E	$23
3E	$23
AE	$23

Santa Jr ... Quick As A Flash
#370104 • Original Price: $20
Issued: 1998 • Retired: 1999

Values

PR	$100
NE	$80

Santa ... Quick As A Flash
(LE-18,000)
#370004 • Original Price: $42
Issued: 1998 • Retired: 1998

New!

Value

NE	$11.50

Shy Bessie Bovine ...
Fresh From The Pasture (LE-2000)
#370058 • Original Price: $11.50
Issued: 2000 • To Be Retired: 2000

Carvers Choice

	Date Purchased	Price Paid	Value
1.			
2.			
3.			
4.			

Totals

1

Values	
1E	$42
2E	$35
3E	$35
AE	$35

Sir Simon Steadfast …
Always Enough Time
#370051 • Original Price: $31
Issued: 1999 • Retired: 1999

2

Value	
NE	N/E

Snortin' Jack Fishbreath …
Carry Out (LE-1999)
#370007 • Original Price: $23
Issued: 1999 • Retired: 1999

3

New!

Value	
NE	$16

Uncle Sammy Leghorn And
George … Rolling Along (LE-2000)
#370057 • Original Price: $16
Issued: 2000 • To Be Retired: 2000

4

Values	
PR	$65
1E	$35
2E	N/E
3E	N/E
AE	N/E

Walter T. Goodlife … Live Well
#370052 • Original Price: $27
Issued: 1999 • Retired: 1999

5

New!

Value	
NE	$16

Wilma Quacksworth With Felix
And Fred … Ridin' High (LE-2000)
#370059 • Original Price: $16
Issued: 2000 • To Be Retired: 2000

Carvers Choice

	Date Purchased	Price Paid	Value
1.			
2.			
3.			
4.			
5.			
Totals			

The Folkstone Collection

Santa & Friends

These jolly Santas were welcomed into the Boyds family in 1994 and honored with retirement three years later (it's hard work being Santa Claus). The collection totals five pieces, each one intricately detailed and entirely festive.

Values	
1E	$130
2E	$85
3E	$70
AE	$50

December 26th
#3003 • Original Price: $33
Issued: 1996 • Retired: 1997

Values	
1E	$110
2E	$67
3E	$55
AE	$47
Variation	
1E	$125
2E	$84
3E	$69
AE	$57

Nick On Ice (GRS)
#3001 • Original Price: $33
Issued: 1994 • Retired: 1997
Variation: original version

Values	
1E	$90
2E	$70
3E	$55
AE	$42
Variation	
1E	$110
2E	$82
3E	$66
AE	$47

Santa's Challenge (GRS)
#3002 • Original Price: $33
Issued: 1994 • Retired: 1997
Variation: original version

Santa & Friends

Date Purchased	Price Paid	Value
1.		
2.		
3.		
4.		

Totals

Values	
1E	$95
2E	$75
3E	$56
AE	$47
Variation	
1E	$122
2E	$85
3E	$73
AE	$55

Santa's Flight Plan (GRS)
#3000 • Original Price: $33
Issued: 1994 • Retired: 1997
Variation: original version

1

Values	
1E	$107
2E	$70
3E	$62
AE	$48
Variation	
1E	$115
2E	$73
3E	$65
AE	$53

Santa's Hobby ...
The Teddy Bear Maker
#3004 • Original Price: $35
Issued: 1996 • Retired: 1997
Variation: 1996 GCC Early Release

The Wee Folkstones

Designed to be placed in nooks and crannies, *The Wee Folkstones* are assorted diminutive angels, faeries and companions who watch over every facet of daily life. Four new guardian angels and mischief makers join the gang this year, bringing their total number to 42.

2

New!

Values	
1E	$19
2E	$19
3E	$19
AE	$19

Amber Faeriedreams ...
Deep In The Forest
#36107 • Original Price: $19
Issued: 2000 • Current

3

Values	
PR	$68
1E	$64
2E	$52
3E	$40
AE	$22

Angelina "Smidge" Angellove ...
Angel Of True Love
#36100 • Original Price: $16
Issued: 1997 • Retired: 1999

4

Values	
JAN	$45
FEB	N/E
MAR	N/E
APR-DEC	N/E

Ann & Abby Angelstitch ...
The Threads That Bind Us (LE-1999)
#36006 • Original Price: $26
Issued: 1999 • Retired: 1999

Santa & Friends

Date Purchased	Price Paid	Value
1.		

The Wee Folkstones

2.		
3.		
4.		

Totals

137

The Folkstone Collection

1

Values	
1E	$36
2E	$19
3E	$19
AE	$19

Arabella & Oscar ... Icy Treats
#36510 • Original Price: $19
Issued: 1999 • Current

2

Values	
1E	$35
2E	$18
3E	$18
AE	$18

Autumn L. Faeriefrost ...
Harvest Time
#36005 • Original Price: $18
Issued: 1999 • Current

3

Values	
1E	$45
2E	$24
3E	$24
AE	$24

Bobby ... The Defender
#36505 • Original Price: $19
Issued: 1998 • Retired: 1999

4

Values	
PR	$55
1E	$50
2E	$25
3E	$25
AE	$19

Caffeinata (Speedy) P. Faeriebean ...
The Coffee Faerie
#36304 • Original Price: $19
Issued: 1998 • Current

The Wee Folkstones

Date Purchased	Price Paid	Value
1.		
2.		
3.		
4.		
5.		

Totals

5

Values	
1E	$42
2E	$24
3E	$24
AE	$18

Cerebella "Smarty" Faerienoggin
#36201 • Original Price: $18
Issued: 1998 • Current

1

Values	
1E	$43
2E	$23
3E	$23
AE	$16

Cicely & Juneau ... Iced Tea Party
#36503 • Original Price: $16
Issued: 1998 • Current

2

Values	
1E	$35
2E	$18
3E	$18
AE	$18

Confidentia "No-Tell" Faeriewhisper
#36105 • Original Price: $18
Issued: 1999 • Current

3

Values	
PR	$58
1E	$46
2E	$34
3E	$22
AE	$18

Dentinata "Faeriefloss" ...
The Tooth Faerie
#36102 • Original Price: $16
Issued: 1997 • Retired: 1999

4

Values	
PR	$55
1E	$52
2E	$40
3E	$35
AE	$18

Electra Angelbyte ...
Angel Of Computer Training
#36300 • Original Price: $18
Issued: 1997 • Current

5

Values	
1E	$50
2E	$38
3E	$33
AE	$28

Estudious "Cram" Faeriebaum ...
The Study Faerie
#36301 • Original Price: $18
Issued: 1997 • Retired: 1999

The Wee Folkstones

	Date Purchased	Price Paid	Value
1.			
2.			
3.			
4.			
5.			

Totals

The Folkstone Collection®

1

Values	
PR	$40
1E	$32
2E	$18
3E	$18
AE	$18

Felicity Angelbliss...
The Bride's Angel
#36103 • Original Price: $18
Issued: 1999 • Current

2

Values	
1E	$32
2E	$18
3E	$18
AE	$18

Fergus "Bogey" MacDivot...
Golf Gnome
#36401 • Original Price: $18
Issued: 1999 • Retired: 1999

3

Values	
1E	$60
2E	$46
3E	$37
AE	$29

Fixit ... Santa's Faerie
#3600 • Original Price: $18
Issued: 1996 • Retired: 1998

4

Values	
1E	$44
2E	$30
3E	$25
AE	$25

Flakey ... Ice Sculptor
#36504 • Original Price: $19
Issued: 1998 • Retired: 1999

The Wee Folkstones

Date Purchased	Price Paid	Value
1.		
2.		
3.		
4.		
5.		

Totals

5

Values	
1E	$40
2E	$19
3E	$19
AE	$19

Florence And Katerina ...
Cold Comfort
#36511 • Original Price: $19
Issued: 1999 • Current

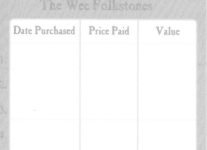

1

Value (U.S.)
NE $65

Flossie Canadian Faerieflosss
(Canadian Exclusive, LE-12,000)
#BC361021 • Original Price: $24.99 (Can.)
Issued: 1997 • Retired: 1999

2

Values
PR $53
1E $43
2E $38
3E $34
AE $29

Gabrielle "Gabby" Faeriejabber ... The
Gossip Faerie
#36003 • Original Price: $18
Issued: 1997 • Retired: 1999

3

Values
PR $38
1E $30
2E $15
3E $15
AE $15

Grandma Faeriehugs
#36106 • Original Price: $15
Issued: 1999 • Current

4

Values
1E $38
2E $27
3E $23
AE $20

Half Pipe ... The Hot Dogger
#36502 • Original Price: $14.50
Issued: 1997 • Retired: 1999

5

Values
1E $32
2E $17
3E $17
AE $17

Henry K. Wallstreet ...
With A Little Bit Of Luck
#36402 • Original Price: $17
Issued: 1999 • Current

The Wee Folkstones

Date Purchased	Price Paid	Value
1.		
2.		
3.		
4.		
5.		
Totals		

The Folkstone Collection

1

Values	
1E	$33
2E	$19
3E	$19
AE	$19

I.B. Freezin'... Iceberg Lettuce
#36508 • Original Price: $19
Issued: 1999 • Current

2

Values	
PR	$60
1E	$55
2E	$42
3E	$35
AE	$18

Immaculata Faerieburg...
The Cleaning Faerie
#36302 • Original Price: $18
Issued: 1997 • Current

3

Values	
PR	$49
1E	$40
2E	$30
3E	$25
AE	$19

Indulgenia Q. Bluit...
Angel Of Denial
#36305 • Original Price: $19
Issued: 1998 • To Be Retired: 2000

4

Values	
1E	$52
2E	$35
3E	$30
AE	$26

Infiniti Faerielove...
The Wedding Faerie
#36101 • Original Price: $16
Issued: 1997 • Retired: 1998

The Wee Folkstones

Date Purchased	Price Paid	Value
1.		
2.		
3.		
4.		

Totals

1

Value	
NE	$47

Katerina & Florence...
Cold Comfort (GCC Exclusive)
#36402GCC • Original Price: $18.50
Issued: 1998 • Retired: 1998

2

Values	
1E	$38
2E	$19
3E	$19
AE	$19

Ketchum & B. Quick... Got One!
#36509 • Original Price: $19
Issued: 1999 • Current

3

Values	
PR	$58
1E	$46
2E	$30
3E	$25
AE	$21

Kristabell Faeriefrost
#36002 • Original Price: $17
Issued: 1997 • Retired: 1999
*Variation: 1997 Premier Edition
"Astriel Faeriefrost"*

4

Values	
PR	$49
1E	$40
2E	$27
3E	$27
AE	$18

Mangianata (Nosh) J. Faeriechild...
The Cooking Faerie
#36303 • Original Price: $18
Issued: 1998 • Current

5

New!

Values	
1E	$19
2E	$19
3E	$19
AE	$19

Mary Angelwish...
May Your Wishes All Come True
#36108 • Original Price: $19
Issued: 2000 • Current

The Wee Folkstones

Date Purchased	Price Paid	Value
1.		
2.		
3.		
4.		
5.		

Totals

The Folkstone Collection

1

Values	
1E	$33
2E	$18
3E	$18
AE	$18

Ms. Picklesencream ...
Heaven's Lil' Blessing
#36202 • Original Price: $18
Issued: 1999 • Current

2

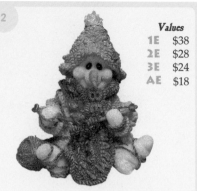

Values	
1E	$38
2E	$28
3E	$24
AE	$18

Pearl ... The Knitter
#36501 • Original Price: $14.50
Issued: 1997 • Retired: 1999

3

Values	
1E	$44
2E	$29
3E	$25
AE	$18

Pearl Too ... The Knitter
#36501-01 • Original Price: $14.50
Issued: 1997 • Retired: 1999

4

New!

Values	
1E	$17
2E	$17
3E	$17
AE	$17

Polly Pekoe ... A Sip Of Tea
#36109 • Original Price: $17
Issued: 2000 • Current

The Wee Folkstones

Date Purchased	Price Paid	Value
1.		
2.		
3.		
4.		
5.		

Totals

5

Values	
PR	$45
1E	$39
2E	$25
3E	$25
AE	$18

Remembrance Angelflyte ...
Time Flies
#36004 • Original Price: $18
Issued: 1998 • Current

1

Values	
1E	$43
2E	$27
3E	$22
AE	$14.50

Slurp And The Snowcone Stand
#36500 • Original Price: $14.50
Issued: 1997 • Current

2

Values (U.S.)	
1E	$46
2E	$14
3E	$14
AE	$14

Stanley The Stick Handler
(Canadian Exclusive)
#BC36507 • Original Price: $20 (Can.)
Issued: 1998 • Current

3

New!

Values	
1E	$19
2E	$19
3E	$19
AE	$19

Sudsie Faeriesock ... Mischief Maker
#36306 • Original Price: $19
Issued: 2000 • Current

4

Values	
1E	$80
2E	$57
3E	$42
AE	$30

T.H. Bean ... The Bearmaker Elf
#36400 • Original Price: $20
Issued: 1997 • Retired: 1999

5

Values	
1E	$32
2E	$18
3E	$18
AE	$18

Tuxworth P. Cummerbund ... The Groom's Angel
#36104 • Original Price: $18
Issued: 1999 • Current

The Wee Folkstones

	Date Purchased	Price Paid	Value
1.			
2.			
3.			
4.			
5.			
Totals			

The Folkstone Collection®

Garden Gang

Both Momma McHopple and Farmer McHare are thrilled to be the first pieces in the newest sub-group of *The Wee Folkstones*. These garden dwellers arrive just in time to help you plant your spring flowers!

New!

Values	
1E	$10
2E	$10
3E	$10
AE	$10

Farmer McHare... Best Intentions
#36601 • Original Price: $10
Issued: 2000 • Current

New!

Values	
1E	$10
2E	$10
3E	$10
AE	$10

**Momma McHopple And Babies...
Naptime**
#36600 • Original Price: $10
Issued: 2000 • Current

Garden Gang

Date Purchased	Price Paid	Value
1.		
2.		
	Totals	

Penguins

Introduced in 1999, this sub-species of *The Wee Folkstones* currently consists of four pieces, including a GCC Early Release. Unofficially called "The Tuxedo Gang," these critters can go from a black-tie ball to a snowball fight at a moments notice.

Values	
1E	$30
2E	$16
3E	$16
AE	$16

Cantwell Waddlewalk & Peek ... Northern Reflections
#36802 • Original Price: $16
Issued: 1999 • Current

Values	
1E	$30
2E	$16
3E	$16
AE	$16

Gaston Coldfin ... The Masterpiece
#36801 • Original Price: $16
Issued: 1999 • Current

Values	
1E	$15.50
2E	$15.50
3E	$15.50
AE	$15.50

Grandma Witefrost ... A Winter's Tale
(GCC Early Release)
#36512GCC • Original Price: $15.50
Issued: 1999 • Current

Values	
1E	$30
2E	$16
3E	$16
AE	$16

Wainwright & Ruby Waddlesworth ...On The Town
#36800 • Original Price: $16
Issued: 1999 • Current

Penguins

	Date Purchased	Price Paid	Value
1.			
2.			
3.			
4.			
		Totals	

Ribbit & Co.

The 11 denizens of the realm of Ribbit (which include three new releases for Spring 2000) are not your average, everyday amphibians. Since their 1998 debut, these frogs have proven to be a hit with collectors who prefer the finer things in life.

	Values
1E	$38
2E	$23
3E	$20
AE	$20

Bridges ... Scuba Frog
#36751 • Original Price: $15
Issued: 1998 • Retired: 1999

	Values
PR	$40
1E	$35
2E	$23
3E	$20
AE	$20

Charles Dunkleburger Prince Of Tales ... Kiss Me Quick!
#36700 • Original Price: $13
Issued: 1998 • Retired: 1999

	Values
PR	$42
1E	$39
2E	$24
3E	$24
AE	$24

Frogmorton And Tad ... Fly Fishing
#36701 • Original Price: $15
Issued: 1998 • Retired: 1999

Ribbit & Co.

Date Purchased	Price Paid	Value
1.		
2.		
3.		
4.		

Totals

	Values
1E	$40
2E	$28
3E	$23
AE	$19

Jacques Grenouille ... The Wine Taster
#36702 • Original Price: $14
Issued: 1998 • Retired: 1998

1

New!

Values	
1E	$15
2E	$15
3E	$15
AE	$15

Jebediah Puddlejump...
What A Drip!
#36706 • Original Price: $15
Issued: 2000 • Current

2

Values	
1E	$33
2E	$25
3E	$20
AE	$16

Jeremiah "Jellybean" Pondhopper
#36704 • Original Price: $14
Issued: 1999 • Retired: 1999

3

New!

Values	
1E	$14
2E	$14
3E	$14
AE	$14

Lloyd Tadpool...Surf's Up
#36708 • Original Price: $14
Issued: 2000 • Current

4

Values	
1E	$30
2E	$14
3E	$14
AE	$14

Ms. Lilypond...Lesson #1
#36705 • Original Price: $14
Issued: 1999 • Current

5

New!

Values	
1E	$14
2E	$14
3E	$14
AE	$14

Princess Puckerup...Kiss Me Quick!
#36707 • Original Price: $14
Issued: 2000 • Current

Ribbit & Co.

Date Purchased	Price Paid	Value
1.		
2.		
3.		
4.		
5.		

Totals

1

Values	
1E	$34
2E	$29
3E	$25
AE	$21

S.C. Ribbit ... Hoppy Christmas
#36750 • Original Price: $14
Issued: 1998 • Retired: 1999

2

Values	
1E	$30
2E	$14
3E	$14
AE	$14

TuTu C. Ribbit ... Frog Lake
#36703 • Original Price: $14
Issued: 1999 • Current

Other Folkstone Collectibles

Three new items have joined the ever-expanding ranks of ornaments, frames, musicals, sconces, votive holders and waterglobes that make up the rest of the Folkstone line.

3

Values	
1E	$40
2E	$24
3E	$24
AE	$21

Barnaby's Snow Sweep Service
Carvers Choice
#370301 • Original Price: $21
Issued: 1998 • Current

Ribbit & Co.

Date Purchased	Price Paid	Value
1.		
2.		

Frames

3.		
4.		

Totals

4

Values	
1E	$40
2E	$35
3E	$32
AE	$28

Darby & Jasper ... Knitten' Kittens
#27451 • Original Price: $21
Issued: 1998 • Retired: 1999

1

Values	
1E	$33
2E	$24
3E	$24
AE	$24

Domestica ... Supermom
#27452 • Original Price: $24
Issued: 1999 • Current

2

Values	
1E	$35
2E	$26
3E	$26
AE	$26

Frogmorton & Tad ... Fly Fishing
Ribbit & Co.
#27402 • Original Price: $24
Issued: 1999 • Retired: 1999

3

Values	
JAN	$45
FEB	$38
MAR	$35
APR-DEC	$32

Liddy Pearl ... They Grow Like Weeds (LE-1998)
#27450 • Original Price: $27
Issued: 1998 • Retired: 1998

4

Values	
1E	$26
2E	$22
3E	$22
AE	$22

Martha Bigheart ... Love Much
Carvers Choice
#370302 • Original Price: $21
Issued: 1999 • Retired: 1999

5

Values	
1E	$38
2E	$23
3E	$23
AE	$21

Santa's Frame Shop
Carvers Choice
#370300 • Original Price: $21
Issued: 1998 • Current

Frames

Date Purchased	Price Paid	Value
1.		
2.		
3.		
4.		
5.		

Totals

The Folkstone Collection

1

New!

Values	
1E	$19
2E	$19
3E	$19
AE	$19

Wendy Willowhare...
A Tisket A Tasket
#27453 • Original Price: $19
Issued: 2000 • Current

2

New!

Values	
1E	$28
2E	$28
3E	$28
AE	$28

Caffeinata "Speedy" P. Faeriebean
♪ *Flashdance*
#271051 • Original Price: $28
Issued: 2000 • Current

3

Values	
1E	$42
2E	$28
3E	$28
AE	$28

Cocoa M. Angelrich And Scoop
The Wee Folkstones
♪ *That's What Friends Are For*
#271050 • Original Price: $28
Issued: 1999 • To Be Retired: 2000

4

Values	
1E	$16
2E	$11
3E	$11
AE	$11

Adoranick... Love Much
Carvers Choice
#370207 • Original Price: $11
Issued: 1999 • Current

5

Values	
1E	$16
2E	$9
3E	$9
AE	$9

Afton... Cross Country
Carvers Choice
#370209 • Original Price: $9
Issued: 1999 • Current

Frames		
Date Purchased	**Price Paid**	**Value**
1.		
Musicals		
2.		
3.		
Ornaments		
4.		
5.		
Totals		

1

Values	
1E	$18
2E	$11
3E	$11
AE	$11

Arlene & Arluck … Pulling Together
Carvers Choice
#370208 • Original Price: $11
Issued: 1999 • Current

2

Values	
1E	$15
2E	$9
3E	$9
AE	$9

Artigo & Avis … Sweet Ride
Carvers Choice
#370210 • Original Price: $9
Issued: 1999 • Current

3

Values	
1E	$18
2E	$10
3E	$10
AE	$10

Avery Frostbuns … Open House
Carvers Choice
#370212 • Original Price: $10
Issued: 1999 • Current

4

Values	
1E	$30
2E	$22
3E	$15
AE	$12

Axel … Thou Shalt Not Melt!
#26562 • Original Price: $12
Issued: 1997 • Retired: 1998

5

Values	
1E	$25
2E	$12
3E	$10
AE	$10

Barnaby … Homeward Bound
Carvers Choice
#370201 • Original Price: $10
Issued: 1998 • Retired: 1999

Ornaments

Date Purchased	Price Paid	Value
1.		
2.		
3.		
4.		
5.		
Totals		

153

The Folkstone Collection

1

Value
NE $25

Birdie...Fore!
#25661 • Original Price: $11
Issued: 1999 • Retired: 1999

2

Values
1E $26
2E $14
3E $10
AE $10

Bjorn...With Nils & Sven
#25654 • Original Price: $12
Issued: 1998 • Current

3

Values
1E $25
2E $14
3E $10
AE $10

Burt...Bundle Up
Carvers Choice
#370202 • Original Price: $10
Issued: 1998 • Retired: 1999

4

Value
NE $25

Chilly With Wreath
#2564 • Original Price: $10
Issued: 1996 • Retired: 1998

Ornaments

Date Purchased	Price Paid	Value
1.		
2.		
3.		
4.		
	Totals	

1

Value	
NE	$30

Father Christmas
#2553 • Original Price: $10
Issued: 1995 • Retired: 1997

2

Values	
1E	$18
2E	$10
3E	$10
AE	$10

I.M. Ketchikan ... Stringin' Along
Carvers Choice
#370214 • Original Price: $10
Issued: 1999 • Current

3

Values	
1E	$30
2E	$20
3E	$15
AE	$12

Ingrid ... Be Warm
#25651 • Original Price: $12
Issued: 1997 • Retired: 1998

4

Values	
1E	$18
2E	$10
3E	$10
AE	$10

J.R. Fairbanks ... Freeze Enterprize
Carvers Choice
#370211 • Original Price: $10
Issued: 1999 • Current

5

Value	
NE	$40

Jacques ... Starlight Skier (LE-1997)
#25950 • Original Price: $21
Issued: 1997 • Retired: 1997

Ornaments

	Date Purchased	Price Paid	Value
1.			
2.			
3.			
4.			
5.			

Totals

155

1

Value
NE $29

Jean Claude & Jacque ... The Skiers
#2561 • Original Price: $10
Issued: 1995 • Retired: 1997

2

Values
1E $18
2E $11
3E $11
AE $11

Jestanick ... Laugh Often
Carvers Choice
#370206 • Original Price: $11
Issued: 1999 • Current

3

Value
NE $38

Jingle Nick (QVC Exclusive)
#63711 • Original Price: N/A
Issued: 1996 • Retired: 1996

4

Value
NE $32

Jingles The Snowman With Wreath
#2562 • Original Price: $10
Issued: 1995 • Retired: 1997

Ornaments

Date Purchased	Price Paid	Value
1.		
2.		
3.		
4.		
5.		

Totals

5

Value
NE $35

Joy (GCC Exclusive)
#25653GCC • Original Price: $10
Issued: 1997 • Retired: 1997

1

Values	
1E	$25
2E	$15
3E	$12
AE	$12

Lars... Ski, Ski, Ski
#25653 • Original Price: $12
Issued: 1998 • Current

2

Value	
NE	$30

Laverne... On Strike
#25659 • Original Price: $11
Issued: 1999 • Retired: 1999

3

Values	
1E	$18
2E	$11
3E	$11
AE	$11

Madge... Magic Scissors
#25658 • Original Price: $11
Issued: 1999 • Current

4

Values	
1E	$30
2E	$11
3E	$11
AE	$11

Mercy... Night Shift
#25656 • Original Price: $11
Issued: 1999 • Current

5

Value	
NE	$40

Mistletoe & Holly –
First Christmas "1997" (LE-1997)
#25900 • Original Price: $14
Issued: 1997 • Retired: 1997

Ornaments

Date Purchased	Price Paid	Value
1.		
2.		
3.		
4.		
5.		

Totals

1

Values	
1E	$18
2E	$11
3E	$11
AE	$11

Ms. Patience … Inspiration
#25657 • Original Price: $11
Issued: 1999 • Current

2

Value	
NE	$30

Myron … The Angler
#25660 • Original Price: $11
Issued: 1999 • Retired: 1999

3

Values	
1E	$35
2E	$24
3E	$21
AE	$21

Nanuk … Winter Wonderland
(LE-1998)
#25956 • Original Price: $21
Issued: 1998 • Retired: 1998

4

Value	
NE	$30

Nicholai With Tree
#2550 • Original Price: $10
Issued: 1995 • Retired: 1997

Ornaments

Date Purchased	Price Paid	Value
1.		
2.		
3.		
4.		

Totals

1

Value	
NE	$30

Nicholas The Giftgiver
#2551 • Original Price: $10
Issued: 1995 • Retired: 1997

2

Value	
NE	$30

Olaf … Let It Snow
#2560 • Original Price: $10
Issued: 1995 • Retired: 1997

3

Values	
1E	$26
2E	$15
3E	$12
AE	$12

Olaf … Let It Snow
#25650 • Original Price: $12
Issued: 1997 • Retired: 1998

4

Values	
1E	$32
2E	$15
3E	$12
AE	$12

Olivia … Wishing You "Peace"
The Wee Folkstones
#25800 • Original Price: $12
Issued: 1998 • Retired: 1999

5

Values	
1E	$18
2E	$11
3E	$11
AE	$11

Ritznick … Live Well
Carvers Choice
#370205 • Original Price: $11
Issued: 1999 • Current

Ornaments

	Date Purchased	Price Paid	Value
1.			
2.			
3.			
4.			
5.			

Totals

The Folkstone Collection

1

Values	
1E	$27
2E	$15
3E	$12
AE	$12

Robin ... Peace On Earth
#25655 • Original Price: $12
Issued: 1998 • Current

2

Values	
1E	$26
2E	$12
3E	$12
AE	$10

Santa ... And The Final Inspection
Carvers Choice
#370203 • Original Price: $10
Issued: 1998 • Retired: 1999

3

Value	
1E	$26
2E	$12
3E	$12
AE	$10

Santa ... In The Nick Of Time
Carvers Choice
#370200 • Original Price: $10
Issued: 1998 • Current

4

Values	
1E	$26
2E	$16
3E	$12
AE	$10

Santa ... Quick As A Flash
Carvers Choice
#370204 • Original Price: $10
Issued: 1998 • Current

Ornaments

Date Purchased	Price Paid	Value
1.		
2.		
3.		
4.		
5.		

Totals

5

Value	
NE	$30

Sliknick In The Chimney
#2552 • Original Price: $10
Issued: 1995 • Retired: 1997

The Folkstone Collection®

1

Value
NE $45

Starry Starry Night
(QVC Exclusive)
#63714 • Original Price: N/A
Issued: 1996 • Retired: 1996

2

Value
NE $20

Willie With Broom
#2565 • Original Price: $10
Issued: 1996 • Retired: 1998

3

Value
NE $25

Windy With Tree
#2563 • Original Price: $10
Issued: 1996 • Retired: 1998

4

Values
1E $38
2E $17
3E $17
AE $17

"Think" Library Book
#65427 • Original Price: $17
Issued: 1998 • Retired: 1999

5

Values
1E $34
2E $27
3E $27
AE $27

Audubon P. Pussywillow …
The Birdwatcher
#27803 • Original Price: $27
Issued: 1999 • Current

Ornaments

	Date Purchased	Price Paid	Value
1.			
2.			
3.			

Sconces

| 4. | | | |

Votive Holders

| 5. | | | |

| | | |

Totals

161

The Folkstone Collection

1

Values	
1E	$30
2E	$27
3E	$27
AE	$27

Cicely & Juneau ... Iced Tea Party
The Wee Folkstones
#27850 • Original Price: $27
Issued: 1999 • Current

2

Values	
1E	$42
2E	$34
3E	$30
AE	$27

Darby & Jasper ... Knitten' Kittens
#27802 • Original Price: $27
Issued: 1998 • Current

3

Values	
1E	$46
2E	$35
3E	$30
AE	$27

Ingrid & Olaf ... Be Warm
#27801 • Original Price: $27
Issued: 1998 • Current

4

New!

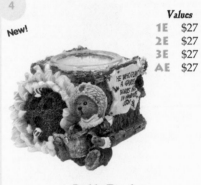

Values	
1E	$27
2E	$27
3E	$27
AE	$27

Liddy Pearl
#27804 • Original Price: $27
Issued: 2000 • Current

Votive Holders

Date Purchased	Price Paid	Value
1.		
2.		
3.		
4.		
5.		

Totals

5

Values	
1E	$48
2E	$40
3E	$30
AE	$27

Yukon & Kodiak ...
Nome Sweet Home
#27800 • Original Price: $27
Issued: 1997 • Retired: 1999

1

Values	
1E	$84
2E	$55
3E	$42
AE	$37

Jean Claude & Jacque ... The Skiers
♪ *Let It Snow*
#2710 • Original Price: $37
Issued: 1996 • Retired: 1998

2

Value	
NE	$78

Liddy Pearl ... How Does Your Garden Grow (LE-1998)
♪ *You Are My Sunshine*
#270602 • Original Price: $53
Issued: 1998 • Retired: 1998

3

Values	
1E	$50
2E	$39
3E	$39
AE	$39

Ms. McFrazzle ... On The Job
#271002 • Original Price: $39
Issued: 1999 • To Be Retired: 2000

4

Value	
NE	$90

Santa's Flight Plan
♪ *Santa Claus Is Coming To Town*
#2703 • Original Price: $36
Issued: 1995 • Retired: 1996

5

Values	
1E	$52
2E	$42
3E	$42
AE	$42

Yukon, Kodiak & Nanuk ... Nome Sweet Home
♪ *White Christmas*
#271001 • Original Price: $39
Issued: 1997 • Retired: 1999

Waterglobes

Date Purchased	Price Paid	Value
1.		
2.		
3.		
4.		
5.		

Totals

163

Folkwear Pins

Keep your guardian angel or faerie close to your heart with a Folkwear pin. For Spring 2000, six new pins were introduced to the collection.

1

Afton...Cross Country
Carvers Choice
Issued: 1999 • Retired
#370508 • **Value: $4**

2

Alice & Emily
Issued: 1996 • Retired
#2666 • **Value: $7**

3

Alison Bear With Jaime Bear
Issued: 1999 • Current
#BC2620PO • **Value: $6.50**

4

Angelina...
Key To My Heart
Issued: 1998 • Retired
#26319 • **Value: $4**

5

Ariel...The Guardian
Issued: 1996 • Retired
#2671 • **Value: $6**

6

Artigo & Avis...Sweet Ride
Carvers Choice
Issued: 1999 • Retired
#370509 • **Value: $4**

7

Ashley The Angel
Issued: 1996 • Retired
#26303 • **Value: $4**

8

Audobon...Birdwatcher
Issued: 1999 • Retired
#26329 • **Value: $4**

9

Auntie Cocoa...
Life Is Short
Issued: 1999 • Retired
#26421 • **Value: $4**

10

Avery Frostbuns...
Open House
Carvers Choice
Issued: 1999 • Retired
#370506 • **Value: $4**

11

Axel...Let It Snow
Issued: 1998 • Retired
#26317 • **Value: $4**

12

Baby Amelia's Carrot Juice
Issued: 1997 • Retired
#26404 • **Value: $8**

13

Barnaby...Homeward Bound
Carvers Choice
Issued: 1998 • Retired
#370501 • **Value: $4**

14

Bearly Santa
Issued: 1997 • Retired
#26311 • **Value: $7**

15

Beatrice's Wreath
Issued: 1995 • Retired
#2638 • **Value: $7**

16

Bessie With Sun Flowers
Issued: 1996 • Retired
#2664 • **Value: N/E**

17

Betty Biscuit
Issued: 1997 • Retired
#26403 • **Value: $8**

18
New!

Calliope Clipsalot...
Guardian Angel Of Pennies
Issued: 2000 • Current
#26424 • **Value: $4**

The Folkstone Collection

Folkwear Pins	Price Paid	Value
1.		
2.		
3.		
4.		
5.		
6.		
7.		
8.		
9.		
10.		
11.		
12.		
13.		
14.		
15.		
16.		
17.		
18.		
Totals		

1

New!

Chester Birdbreath …
What Bird?
Issued: 2000 • Current
#26429 • *Value: $4*

2

Daphne In Straw Hat
Issued: 1996 • Retired
#2668 • *Value: $8*

3

Domestica … Supermom
Issued: 1999 • Retired
#26330 • *Value: $6*

4

Dr. Mooselberry …
Making Rounds
Issued: 1999 • Retired
#26327 • *Value: $6*

5

Egads … The Skier
Issued: 1997 • Retired
#26308 • *Value: $8*

6

Electronick … Unplugged
Issued: 1999 • Retired
#26322 • *Value: $4*

7

Eloise In The Cabbage Patch
Issued: 1996 • Retired
#2661 • *Value: $4*

8

Eloise … Tea Toter
Issued: 1997 • Retired
#26402 • *Value: $8*

9

Esmeralda The Witch
Issued: 1996 • Retired
#26304 • *Value: $10*

10

Felicia … Angel Cat
Issued: 1999 • Retired
#26324 • *Value: $6*

11

Fenton J. Padworthy …
The Formal Frog
Issued: 1998 • Retired
#26412 • *Value: $8*

12

Flora … Hoppy Spring
Issued: 1999 • Retired
#26418 • *Value: $4*

13

Florence Wings It
Issued: 1995 • Retired
#2625 • *Value: $8*

14

Florina's Wreath
Issued: 1997 • Retired
#26400 • *Value: $8*

15

"Flossie" … Keep Smiling
Issued: 1998 • Retired
#26411 • *Value: $6*

16

Frogmorton …
Fish, Lie, Fish
Issued: 1999 • Retired
#26415 • *Value: $4*

17

Frogmorton …
Pad Sweet Pad
Issued: 1998 • Retired
#26414 • *Value: $6*

18

Frosty Kristabell
Issued: 1997 • Retired
#26309 • *Value: $7*

19

Fuzznick With Claws & Co.
Issued: 1999 • Retired
#26323 • *Value: $4*

20

Harriet … Farm Fresh
Issued: 1999 • Retired
#26423 • *Value: $4*

Folkwear Pins

	Price Paid	Value
1.		
2.		
3.		
4.		
5.		
6.		
7.		
8.		
9.		
10.		
11.		
12.		
13.		
14.		
15.		
16.		
17.		
18.		
19.		
20.		

Totals

1

New!

Heather...Guardian Angel
Of Volleyball
Issued: 2000 • Current
#26425 • *Value:* $4

2

Helga...Be Warm
Issued: 1998 • Retired
#26318 • *Value:* $4

3

New!

Honker T. Flatfoot...
Send In The Clowns
Issued: 2000 • Current
#26426 • *Value:* $4

4

I.M. Ketchikan...
Stringin' Along
Carvers Choice
Issued: 1999 • Retired
#370507 • *Value:* $4

5

Immaculata...Scrub-A-Dub!
Issued: 1999 • Retired
#26422 • *Value:* $4

6

J.R. Fairbanks...
Freeze Enterprize
Carvers Choice
Issued: 1999 • Retired
#370505 • *Value:* $4

7

Jasper...Knittin' Kitten
Issued: 1999 • Retired
#26417 • *Value:* $4

8

Jean Claude The Skier
Issued: 1995 • Retired
#2651 • *Value:* $8

9

New!

Jebediah Puddlejump...
What A Drip!
Issued: 2000 • Current
#26427 • *Value:* $4

10

Jingles With Wreath
Issued: 1996 • Retired
#26302 • *Value:* $8

11

Lars...Bells Are Ringing
Issued: 1997 • Retired
#26306 • *Value:* $7

12

Madge...
Beautician/Magician
Issued: 1998 • Retired
#26406 • *Value:* $7

13

McDivot...Golf, Lie, Golf
Issued: 1998 • Retired
#26409 • *Value:* $6

14

Melvin...The Jingle Moose
Issued: 1997 • Retired
#26307 • *Value:* $9

15

Minerva With Daffodils
Issued: 1996 • Retired
#2658 • *Value:* $4

16

Minerva's Flight
Issued: 1995 • Retired
#2647 • *Value:* $10

17

Ms. McFrazzle...Care Giver
Issued: 1999 • Retired
#26420 • *Value:* $4

18

Ms. Patience...Teach, Learn
Issued: 1998 • Retired
#26405 • *Value:* $4

19

Ms. Patience...The Teacher
Issued: 1997 • Retired
#26401 • *Value:* $8

Folkwear Pins

	Price Paid	Value
1.		
2.		
3.		
4.		
5.		
6.		
7.		
8.		
9.		
10.		
11.		
12.		
13.		
14.		
15.		
16.		
17.		
18.		
19.		

Totals

1

Ms. Prudence...Teach, Learn
Issued: 1999 • Retired
#26416 • *Value:* **$4**

2

Murphy...Fire & Ice
Issued: 1999 • Retired
#26328 • *Value:* **$4**

3

Nana & Aubergine & Peapod
Issued: 1998 • Retired
#26407 • *Value:* **$4**

4

Na-Nick Of The North
Issued: 1995 • Retired
#2650 • *Value:* **$4**

5

Nicholai...With Dove
Issued: 1995 • Retired
#2648 • *Value:* **$10**

6

Nicholai With Tree
Issued: 1996 • Retired
#26300 • *Value:* **$10**

7

Nicholas Tacklebox...
Frozen Fish
Carvers Choice
Issued: 1999 • Retired
#370510 • *Value:* **$4**

8

Nicholas...With Tree
Issued: 1995 • Retired
#2649 • *Value:* **$10**

9

Nome Sweet Home
Issued: 1997 • Retired
#26310 • *Value:* **$7**

10

"Nosh"...
What's Cooking?!?!
Issued: 1998 • Retired
#26408 • *Value:* **$6**

11

Oceania
Issued: 1996 • Retired
#2674 • *Value:* **$8**

12

Olaf...I Luuv Snow
Issued: 1998 • Retired
#26321 • *Value:* **$4**

13

Olaf...
The Flakey Snowman
Issued: 1997 • Retired
#26305 • *Value:* **$8**

14

Peacenik Santa
Issued: 1997 • Retired
#26314 • *Value:* **$8**

15
New!

Princess Puckerup...
Kiss Me Quick!
Issued: 2000 • Current
#26428 • *Value:* **$4**

16

Purrscilla & Friends
Issued: 1999 • Retired
#26419 • *Value:* **$4**

17

Ralph Angel Pooch
Issued: 1996 • Retired
#2669 • *Value:* **$7**

18

Sabrina...
Bippity Boppity Boo!
Issued: 1998 • Retired
#26315 • *Value:* **$4**

19

Santa...
And The Final Inspection
Carvers Choice
Issued: 1998 • Retired
#370503 • *Value:* **$4**

20

Santa Claws
Issued: 1999 • Retired
#26325 • *Value:* **$6**

Folkwear Pins

	Price Paid	Value
1.		
2.		
3.		
4.		
5.		
6.		
7.		
8.		
9.		
10.		
11.		
12.		
13.		
14.		
15.		
16.		
17.		
18.		
19.		
20.		
Totals		

The Folkstone Collection

1

Santa...
In The Nick Of Time
Carvers Choice
Issued: 1998 • Retired
#370500 • *Value:* **$4**

2

Santa... Quick As A Flash
Carvers Choice
Issued: 1998 • Retired
#370504 • *Value:* **$4**

3

Santoad
Issued: 1998 • Retired
#26320 • *Value:* **$4**

4

Siegfried The Santa Moose
Issued: 1995 • Retired
#2653 • *Value:* **$16**

5

Sliknick On The Chimney
Issued: 1996 • Retired
#26301 • *Value:* **$10**

6

Slurp... 5¢ A Lick
Issued: 1998 • Retired
#26316 • *Value:* **$4**

7

"Speedy"... Fast As I Can!
Issued: 1998 • Retired
#26410 • *Value:* **$6**

8

"Too Loose" Lapin
Issued: 1996 • Retired
#2665 • *Value:* **$4**

Folkwear Pins

	Price Paid	Value
1.		
2.		
3.		
4.		
5.		
6.		
7.		
8.		
9.		
10.		
11.		

9

Willie With Evergreens
Issued: 1997 • Retired
#26312 • *Value:* **$7**

10

Windy The Snowman
Issued: 1995 • Retired
#2652 • *Value:* **$4**

11

Zambonie... Got Snow?
Issued: 1999 • Retired
#26326 • *Value:* **$6**

The Purrstone Collection

Cats in all their playful glory are celebrated in this new resin collection. Making their debut in 1999 with six pieces, this group added seven more pieces for Spring 2000, proving that collectors just can't get enough of these friendly felines.

1

New!

Values	
PR	$40
1E	$17
2E	$17
3E	$17
AE	$17

Chester Birdbreath ... What Bird?
#371006 • Original Price: $17
Issued: 2000 • Current

2

Values	
PR	$40
1E	$30
2E	$17
3E	$17
AE	$17

**Clawdette Fuzzface & Wuly ...
Yarn Merchants**
#371002 • Original Price: $17
Issued: 1999 • Current

3

New!

Values	
1E	$15
2E	$15
3E	$15
AE	$15

**Dominique Surefoot With Coach
Colby ... Practice Makes Purrfect**
#371052 • Original Price: $15
Issued: 2000 • Current

4

Values	
PR	$40
1E	$30
2E	$17.50
3E	$17.50
AE	$17.50

**Felicia Angelpuss & George ...
Peace On Earth**
#371004 • Original Price: $17.50
Issued: 1999 • Current

General Figurines

	Date Purchased	Price Paid	Value
1.			
2.			
3.			
4.			

Totals

The Purrstone Collection™

1 New!

Values	
1E	$18
2E	$18
3E	$18
AE	$18

Kandace Purrshop...
Hidden Surprises
#371054 • Original Price: $18
Issued: 2000 • Current

2

Values	
PR	$32
1E	$25
2E	$16
3E	$16
AE	$16

Maddie Purrkins With Puddytat...
Cat Nap
#371001 • Original Price: $16
Issued: 1999 • Current

3 New!

Values	
1E	$19
2E	$19
3E	$19
AE	$19

Mama Purrsmore And Baby Belle
With Rinky, Dinky and Dew...
Once Upon A Time
#371053 • Original Price: $19
Issued: 2000 • Current

4

Values	
JAN	$55
FEB	$27
MAR	$27
APR-DEC	$27

Mrs. Fezziwig With Marley, Bob &
Caroline... Caterwauling (LE-1999)
#371005 • Original Price: $27
Issued: 1999 • Retired: 1999

General Figurines

	Date Purchased	Price Paid	Value
1.			
2.			
3.			
4.			
	Totals		

1 New!

Values (U.S.)	
1E	$18.50
2E	$18.50
3E	$18.50
AE	$18.50

Nadia Surefoot With Coach Muenster (Canadian Exclusive)
#BC371055PO • Original Price: $26.99 (Can.)
Issued: 2000 • Current

2 New!

Values	
1E	$19
2E	$19
3E	$19
AE	$19

Opie Baithook With Barney ... Catch Of The Day
#371051 • Original Price: $19
Issued: 2000 • Current

3

Values	
1E	$30
2E	$15
3E	$15
AE	$15

Pawlene Prowler ... Spooky Treats
#371000 • Original Price: $15
Issued: 1999 • Current

4 New!

Values	
1E	$20.50
2E	$20.50
3E	$20.50
AE	$20.50

Pokie Pawsworthy ... The Bug Inspector
#371050 • Original Price: $20.50
Issued: 2000 • Current

5

Values	
PR	$45
1E	$35
2E	$17
3E	$17
AE	$17

Santa Claws & Nibbles ... A Purrfect Holiday
#371003 • Original Price: $17
Issued: 1999 • Current

General Figurines

	Date Purchased	Price Paid	Value
1.			
2.			
3.			
4.			
5.			
Totals			

171

The Dollstone Collection

This collection depicts the large and small events in a child's life, a charming reminder of the innocence and wonder of childhood. With seven new figurines available for Spring 2000, there just might be one that reminds you of a special child in your life.

1

Values	
PR	$50
1E	$32
2E	$18
3E	$18
AE	$18

Alyssa With Caroline... A Stitch In Time
#3539 • Original Price: $18
Issued: 1999 • Current

2

Values	
PR	$155
JAN	$118
FEB	$92
MAR	$84
APR-DEC	$70

The Amazing Bailey... "Magic Show At 4" (LE-1997)
#3518 • Original Price: $58
Issued: 1997 • Retired: 1997

3

Values	
PR	$75
1E	$65
2E	$45
3E	$36
AE	$30

Amy And Edmund... Momma's Clothes
#3529 • Original Price: $30
Issued: 1998 • Current

General Figurines

	Date Purchased	Price Paid	Value
1.			
2.			
3.			
4.			
		Totals	

4

Values	
1E	$86
2E	$58
3E	$42
AE	$29

Anne... The Masterpiece
#3599 • Original Price: $25
Issued: 1996 • Retired: 1999

1

Values	
PR	$88
1E	$77
2E	$50
3E	$39
AE	$33

Ashley With Chrissie ... Dress Up
#3506 • Original Price: $20.50
Issued: 1996 • Retired: 1999

2

Values	
PR	$65
1E	$60
2E	$47
3E	$35
AE	$28

"THE CHIEF"

Austin & Allen ... The Fire Chief
#3534 • Original Price: $20
Issued: 1998 • Retired: 1999

3

New!

Values	
1E	$24
2E	$24
3E	$24
AE	$24

Barbara Ann With Jodi And Annie ... Stitched With Love
#3554 • Original Price: $24
Issued: 2000 • Current

4

Values	
PR	$78
1E	$68
2E	$46
3E	$36
AE	$29

STOP

Benjamin With Matthew ... The Speed Trap
#3524 • Original Price: $29
Issued: 1997 • To Be Retired: 2000

5

Values (U.S.)	
1E	$83
2E	$72
3E	$52
AE	$38

Betsey And Edmund With Union Jack (Canadian Exclusive)
#BC35031 • Original Price: $29.99 (Can.)
Issued: 1996 • Current

General Figurines

	Date Purchased	Price Paid	Value
1.			
2.			
3.			
4.			
5.			

Totals

Yesterday's Child • The Dollstone Collection™

1

Values	
PR	$165
1E	$99
2E	$61
3E	$47
AE	$20

Betsey With Edmund ... The Patriots
#3503 • Original Price: $20
Issued: 1996 • To Be Retired: 2000

2

New!

Values	
1E	$20
2E	$20
3E	$20
AE	$20

Brooke With Joshua ... Puddle Jumpers
#3551 • Original Price: $20
Issued: 2000 • Current

3

Values	
PR	$70
1E	$62
2E	$45
3E	$38
AE	$24

Caitlin With Emma & Edmund ... Diapering Baby
#3525 • Original Price: $20
Issued: 1997 • Retired: 1999

4

Value	
NE	$78

PHOTO UNAVAILABLE

Caitlin With Emma & Edmund ... Diapering Baby (Kirlin's Exclusive)
#3525-1 • Original Price: $20
Issued: 1997 • Retired: 1998

General Figurines

	Date Purchased	Price Paid	Value
1.			
2.			
3.			
4.			
5.			

Totals

5

Values	
PR	$88
1E	$85
2E	$54
3E	$48
AE	$40

Candice With Matthew ... Gathering Apples
#3514 • Original Price: $19
Issued: 1996 • Retired: 1999

1

New!

Values	
JAN	$36
FEB	$36
MAR	$36
APR-DEC	$36

Casey With Baxter...
Afternoon Stroll (LE-2000)
#3557 • Original Price: $36
Issued: 2000 • To Be Retired: 2000

2

Values	
PR	$50
1E	$40
2E	$20
3E	$20
AE	$20

Cheryl With Ashlie...
Nighty Night
#3544 • Original Price: $20
Issued: 1999 • Current

3

New!

Values	
1E	$14
2E	$14
3E	$14
AE	$14

Cindy With Collier...Dress Up
#3555 • Original Price: $14
Issued: 2000 • Current

4

Values	
1E	$85
2E	$57
3E	$52
AE	$38

Courtney With Phoebe...Over The
River And Thru The Woods
#3512 • Original Price: $25
Issued: 1996 • Retired: 1997

5

Values	
1E	$109
2E	$88
3E	$74
AE	$48

Courtney With Phoebe...Over The
River And Thru The Woods
(GCC Exclusive)
#3512-01 • Original Price: $27.50
Issued: 1996 • Retired: 1996

General Figurines

	Date Purchased	Price Paid	Value
1.			
2.			
3.			
4.			
5.			

Totals

1

Value	
NE	$200

Elizabeth And Gary
(LE-25,000, QVC Exclusive,
porcelain doll and figurine set)
#4911V • Original Price: $116
Issued: 1998 • Retired: 1998

2

Values	
PR	$122
1E	$90
2E	$60
3E	$53
AE	$30

Emily With Kathleen & Otis...
The Future
#3508 • Original Price: $30
Issued: 1996 • Current

3

Values	
PR	$45
1E	$38
2E	$20
3E	$20
AE	$20

Heather With Lauren...
Bunny Helpers
#3538 • Original Price: $20
Issued: 1999 • Current

4

Values	
PR	$68
1E	$55
2E	$42
3E	$33
AE	$20

Jamie And Thomasina...
The Last One
#3530 • Original Price: $20
Issued: 1998 • Current

General Figurines

	Date Purchased	Price Paid	Value
1.			
2.			
3.			
4.			
5.			

Totals

5

Values	
PR	$75
1E	$66
2E	$50
3E	$36
AE	$27

Jean With Elliot & Debbie...
The Bakers
#3510 • Original Price: $20
Issued: 1996 • Retired: 1999

Value Guide — Boyds Bears & Friends™

1

	Value
NE	$95

Jean With Elliot & Debbie...
The Bakers (Kirlin's Exclusive)
#3510-01 • Original Price: $19
Issued: 1996 • Retired: 1996

2

	Values
PR	$225
1E	$100
2E	$65
3E	$49
AE	$37

Jennifer With Priscilla...
The Doll In The Attic
#3500 • Original Price: $20.50
Issued: 1996 • Retired: 1997

3

	Values
JAN	$100
FEB	$69
MAR	$53
APR-DEC	$48

Jessica And Timmy...
Animal Hospital (LE-1998)
#3532 • Original Price: $40
Issued: 1998 • Retired: 1998

4

	Values
PR	$73
1E	$60
2E	$42
3E	$35
AE	$20

Julia With Emmy Lou & Daphne...
Garden Friends
#3520 • Original Price: $20
Issued: 1997 • Current

5

	Values
1E	$68
2E	$55
3E	$40
AE	$32

Karen With Wilson & Eloise...
Mother's Present
#3515-01 • Original Price: $20
Issued: 1997 • Retired: 1998

General Figurines

	Date Purchased	Price Paid	Value
1.			
2.			
3.			
4.			
5.			

Totals

1

	Values
1E	$79
2E	$60
3E	$50
AE	$36

Karen With Wilson & Eloise...
Mother's Present (GCC Exclusive)
#3515GCC • Original Price: $26
Issued: 1996 • Retired: 1996

2

	Values
PR	$175
1E	$95
2E	$70
3E	$50
AE	$20

Katherine With Edmund
& Amanda... Kind Hearts
#3505 • Original Price: $20
Issued: 1996 • Current

3

	Values
JAN	$78
FEB	$54
MAR	$49
APR-DEC	$45

Kelly And Company...
The Bear Collector (LE-1999)
#3542 • Original Price: $36
Issued: 1999 • Retired: 1999

4

	Values
PR	$48
1E	$40
2E	$18
3E	$18
AE	$18

Kimberly With Klaus...
Special Delivery
#3547 • Original Price: $18
Issued: 1999 • Current

5

	Values
1E	$68
2E	$52
3E	$40
AE	$30
	Variation
NE	$87

Kristi With Nicole... Skater's Waltz
#3516 • Original Price: $26
Issued: 1996 • Retired: 1999
Variation: 1996 GCC Early Release

General Figurines

	Date Purchased	Price Paid	Value
1.			
2.			
3.			
4.			
5.			

Totals

Value Guide — Boyds Bears & Friends™

1

Values	
PR	$77
1E	$60
2E	$40
3E	$35
AE	$23

Laura With Jane...
First Day Of School
#3522 • Original Price: $23
Issued: 1997 • To Be Retired: 2000

2

Values	
PR	$66
1E	$48
2E	$36
3E	$27
AE	$18

Lindsey With Louise...The Recital
#3535 • Original Price: $18
Issued: 1998 • Current

3

New!

Values	
1E	$18
2E	$18
3E	$18
AE	$18

Lisa With Plato...Graduation Day
#3550 • Original Price: $18
Issued: 2000 • Current

4

Values	
1E	$30
2E	$18
3E	$18
AE	$18

Lucinda And Dawn...By The Sea
#3536 • Original Price: $18
Issued: 1999 • Current

5

Values	
PR	$170
1E	$90
2E	$65
3E	$48
AE	$34

Mallory With Patsy & J.B. Bean...
Trick Or Treat
#3517 • Original Price: $27
Issued: 1996 • Retired: 1999

General Figurines

	Date Purchased	Price Paid	Value
1.			
2.			
3.			
4.			
5.			

Totals

1

Values	
PR	$50
1E	$38
2E	$14
3E	$14
AE	$14

Mark With Luke ... The Prayer
#3545 • Original Price: $14
Issued: 1999 • To Be Retired: 2000

2

Value	
NE	$165

Mary And Paul ... The Prayer
(LE-1998, G.M's Choice)
#3531-01 • Original Price: $16
Issued: 1998 • Retired: 1998

3

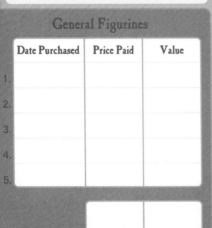

Values	
PR	$350
1E	$90
2E	$58
3E	$48
AE	$30

Megan With Elliot And Annie ...
Christmas Carol
#3504 • Original Price: $20
Issued: 1996 • Retired: 1999

4

Values	
PR	$50
1E	$35
2E	$18
3E	$18
AE	$18

Melissa With Katie ... The Ballet
#3537 • Original Price: $18
Issued: 1999 • Current

General Figurines

	Date Purchased	Price Paid	Value
1.			
2.			
3.			
4.			
5.			
	Totals		

5

Values	
1E	$45
2E	$30
3E	$26
AE	$22

Meredith With Jacqueline ...
Daisy Chain
#3541 • Original Price: $18
Issued: 1999 • Retired: 1999

Value Guide — Boyds Bears & Friends™

1

Values	
PR	$50
1E	$36
2E	$20
3E	$20
AE	$20

Mia … The Save
#3549 • Original Price: $20
Issued: 1999 • Current

2

New!

Values	
1E	$25
2E	$25
3E	$25
AE	$25

**Michael And Thayer …
Waitin' For Grandpa**
#3552 • Original Price: $25
Issued: 2000 • Current

3

Values	
PR	$75
1E	$66
2E	$48
3E	$34
AE	$18

**Michelle With Daisy …
Reading Is Fun**
#3511 • Original Price: $18
Issued: 1996 • Current

4

Values	
PR	$75
1E	$60
2E	$37
3E	$37
AE	$37

**Miranda With Mary K.…
Pretty As A Picture**
#3548 • Original Price: $37
Issued: 1999 • Current

5

Values	
1E	$74
2E	$55
3E	$45
AE	$32

Natalie With Joy … Sunday School
#3519 • Original Price: $23
Issued: 1997 • Retired: 1999

General Figurines

	Date Purchased	Price Paid	Value
1.			
2.			
3.			
4.			
5.			

Totals

181

1

Values	
PR	$220
1E	$89
2E	$66
3E	$50
AE	$24

Patricia With Molly ...
Attic Treasures
#3501 • Original Price: $14
Issued: 1996 • Retired: 1999

2

Values	
PR	$50
JAN	$38
FEB	$14
MAR	$14
APR-DEC	$14

Peter With James ... The Prayer
(LE-1999, G.M.'s Choice)
#3545-06 • Original Price: $14
Issued: 1999 • Retired: 1999

3

Values	
1E	$70
2E	$48
3E	$35
AE	$29

Rachael, Barbara & Matthew ...
Sabbath Lights
#3526 • Original Price: $23
Issued: 1998 • Retired: 1999

4

Values	
PR	$92
1E	$69
2E	$50
3E	$43
AE	$21

Rebecca With Elliot ... Birthday
#3509 • Original Price: $21
Issued: 1996 • To Be Retired: 2000

General Figurines

	Date Purchased	Price Paid	Value
1.			
2.			
3.			
4.			
5.			

Totals

5

New!

Values	
1E	$30
2E	$30
3E	$30
AE	$30

Ryan & Diane With Cory, Wesley
And Carly ... Love Is Forever
#3553 • Original Price: $30
Issued: 2000 • Current

Value Guide — Boyds Bears & Friends™

1

Values	
1E	$80
2E	$63
3E	$52
AE	$45
Variation	
PR	$110

Sandra Claus... Christmas Morning
#3528-1 • Original Price: $39
Issued: 1998 • Retired: 1999
Variation: "Sandy Claus"

2

Values	
PR	$170
JAN	$130
FEB	$105
MAR	$90
APR-DEC	$75

Sarah & Heather With Elliot, Dolly & Amelia... Tea For Four (LE-1996)
#3507 • Original Price: $47
Issued: 1996 • Retired: 1996

3

Values	
PR	$85
1E	$77
2E	$58
3E	$48
AE	$34

Shannon & Wilson... Wait'n For Grandma
#3533 • Original Price: $34
Issued: 1998 • Current

4

Values	
PR	$63
1E	$45
2E	$38
3E	$30
AE	$15

Shelby... Asleep In Teddy's Arms
#3527 • Original Price: $15
Issued: 1998 • To Be Retired: 2000

5

Values	
PR	$50
1E	$42
2E	$26
3E	$26
AE	$26

Stephanie With Jim... School Days
#3540 • Original Price: $26
Issued: 1999 • Current

General Figurines

	Date Purchased	Price Paid	Value
1.			
2.			
3.			
4.			
5.			

Totals

1

Values	
PR	$50
1E	$40
2E	$20
3E	$20
AE	$20

Tami With Doug... Half Time
#3546 • Original Price: $20
Issued: 1999 • To Be Retired: 2000

2

Values	
PR	$55
1E	$42
2E	$35
3E	$29
AE	$14

Teresa And John... The Prayer
#3531 • Original Price: $14
Issued: 1998 • Current

3

Values	
PR	$165
1E	$92
2E	$75
3E	$62
AE	$36

Victoria With Samantha...
Victorian Ladies
#3502 • Original Price: $20
Issued: 1996 • Retired: 1999

4

Values	
PR	$93
1E	$80
2E	$59
3E	$50
AE	$39

Wendy With Bronte, Keats,
Tennyson & Poe...Wash Day
#3521 • Original Price: $23
Issued: 1997 • Retired: 1998

General Figurines

	Date Purchased	Price Paid	Value
1.			
2.			
3.			
4.			
5.			

Totals

5

Values	
1E	$57
2E	$52
3E	$40
AE	$20

Whitney With Wilson... Tea Party
#3523 • Original Price: $20
Issued: 1997 • Current

Other Dollstone Collectibles

The Dollstone Collection includes a variety of child-themed frames, votive holders, musicals, ornaments and water-globes, as well as an adorable assortment of San Francisco Music Boxes.

Values	
PR	$45
1E	$30
2E	$17
3E	$17
AE	$17

Laura With Jane... First Day Of School
#27552 • Original Price: $17
Issued: 1999 • To Be Retired: 2000

Values	
1E	$40
2E	$32
3E	$27
AE	$27

Lindsey With Louise... The Recital
#27551 • Original Price: $24
Issued: 1999 • Retired: 1999

Values	
1E	$45
2E	$28
3E	$28
AE	$25

Tiffany... "Forever"
#27550 • Original Price: $25
Issued: 1998 • To Be Retired: 2000

Values	
1E	$72
2E	$45
3E	$45
AE	$37

Emily With Kathleen & Otis... The Future
♪ *Wagner's Wedding March*
#272052 • Original Price: $37
Issued: 1998 • Current

Frames		
Date Purchased	Price Paid	Value
1.		
2.		
3.		

Musicals		
4.		

Totals

185

Yesterday's Child • The Dollstone Collection™

1

	Values	
1E	$60
2E	$40
3E	$40
AE	$40

Grace & Faith ... I Have A Dream
♪ *You've Got A Friend*
#272054 • Original Price: $37
Issued: 1999 • Retired: 1999

2

	Values	
PR	N/E
1E	$50
2E	$37
3E	$37
AE	$37

Melissa With Katie & Desiree ... The Ballet
♪ *Music Box Dancer*
#272003 • Original Price: $37
Issued: 1999 • Current

3

New!

	Values	
1E	$37
2E	$37
3E	$37
AE	$37

Miranda And Robert ... Put On A Happy Face
♪ *Put On A Happy Face*
#272055 • Original Price: $37
Issued: 2000 • Current

4

	Values	
PR	$84
1E	$76
2E	$63
3E	$46
AE	$37

Whitney With Wilson ... Tea Party
♪ *Tea For Two*
#272001 • Original Price: $37
Issued: 1997 • Current

Musicals

	Date Purchased	Price Paid	Value
1.			
2.			
3.			
4.			

Ornaments

5.			

Totals

5

	Values	
JAN	$22
FEB	$12
MAR	$12
APR-DEC	$12

Amy & Sam ... Baby's First Christmas (LE-1999)
#25857 • Original Price: $12
Issued: 1999 • Retired: 1999

1

Values	
1E	$22
2E	$11
3E	$11
AE	$11

Betsy ... The Patriot
#25854 • Original Price: $11
Issued: 1999 • Retired: 1999

2

Value	
NE	$13

Candice With Matthew ... Gathering Apples
#25851 • Original Price: $10
Issued: 1998 • Retired: 1999

3

Value	
NE	$13

Jean With Elliot ... The Bakers
#25852 • Original Price: $10
Issued: 1998 • Retired: 1999

4

Values	
1E	$22
2E	$11
3E	$11
AE	$11

Katherine ... Kind Heart
#25853 • Original Price: $11
Issued: 1999 • Retired: 1999

5

Value	
NE	$12

Megan With Elliot ... Christmas Carol
#25850 • Original Price: $10
Issued: 1998 • Retired: 1999

Ornaments

	Date Purchased	Price Paid	Value
1.			
2.			
3.			
4.			
5.			
Totals			

187

1

Values	
1E	$22
2E	$11
3E	$11
AE	$11

Michelle ... Reading Is Fun
#25855 • Original Price: $11
Issued: 1999 • Retired: 1999

2

Values	
JAN	$25
FEB	$12
MAR	$12
APR-DEC	$12

Ryan & Diane ... Love Is Forever
(LE-1999)
#25856 • Original Price: $12
Issued: 1999 • Retired: 1999

3

Values	
JAN	$25
FEB	$12
MAR	$12
APR-DEC	$12

Shannon ... Christmas At Grandma's
(LE-1999)
#25858 • Original Price: $12
Issued: 1999 • Retired: 1999

4

Values	
1E	$45
2E	$27
3E	$27
AE	$27

Candice With Matthew ...
Gathering Apples
#27901 • Original Price: $27
Issued: 1999 • To Be Retired: 2000

5

Values	
PR	N/E
1E	$50
2E	$35
3E	$27
AE	$27

Lucinda And Dawn ... By The Sea
#27951 • Original Price: $27
Issued: 1999 • Current

Ornaments

	Date Purchased	Price Paid	Value
1.			
2.			
3.			

Votive Holders

4.			
5.			

Totals

Value Guide — Boyds Bears & Friends™

1

Values	
1E	$50
2E	$32
3E	$25
AE	$20

Teresa & John ... The Prayer
#27900 • Original Price: $20
Issued: 1998 • Current

2

Values	
1E	$62
2E	$48
3E	$40
AE	$30

Whitney With Wilson ... Tea And Candlelight
#27950 • Original Price: $26
Issued: 1997 • Retired: 1999

3

New!

Values	
1E	$38
2E	$38
3E	$38
AE	$38

Kelly And Company ... The Bear Collector
♪ *Let Me Be Your Teddy Bear*
#272056 • Original Price: $38
Issued: 2000 • Current

4

Values	
1E	$50
2E	$38
3E	$38
AE	$38

Lindsey With Louis ... The Recital
♪ *Fur Elise*
#272002 • Original Price: $38
Issued: 1999 • Current

5

Values	
1E	$95
2E	$78
3E	$60
AE	$47

Megan With Elliot ... Christmas Carol
(limited to one year of production)
♪ *Amazing Grace*
#2720 • Original Price: $39
Issued: 1996 • Retired: 1997

Votive Holders

	Date Purchased	Price Paid	Value
1.			
2.			

Waterglobes

	Date Purchased	Price Paid	Value
3.			
4.			
5.			

Totals

Yesterday's Child • The Dollstone Collection™

1

Values	
1E	$50
2E	$38
3E	$38
AE	$38

Ryan & Diane ... Love Is Forever
♪ *Love Is A Many Splendored Thing*
#272053 • Original Price: $38
Issued: 1999 • Current

2

Values	
1E	$100
2E	$85
3E	$85
AE	$85

Brittany II ... Life's Journey
♪ *The Long And Winding Road*
#4906SF • Original Price: $85
Issued: 1999 • Current

3

Values	
PR	N/E
1E	$105
2E	$88
3E	$70
AE	$50

Gardening Friends
♪ *Where Have All The Flowers Gone?*
#2776SF • Original Price: $50
Issued: 1999 • Current

4

Values	
PR	N/E
1E	$98
2E	$65
3E	$45
AE	$45

Goin' To Grandma's
♪ *It's A Long Way To Tipperary*
#2775SF • Original Price: $45
Issued: 1999 • Retired: 1999

5

Values	
1E	N/E
2E	$55
3E	$55
AE	$55

Momma's Clothes
♪ *Thank Heaven For Little Girls*
#2781SF • Original Price: $55
Issued: 1999 • To Be Retired: 2000

Waterglobes		
Date Purchased	**Price Paid**	**Value**
1.		

San Francisco Music Boxes		
2.		
3.		
4.		
5.		

Totals		

1

Values
1E N/E
2E $55
3E $55
AE $55

School Days
♪ *I'd Like To Teach The World To Sing*
#2783SF • Original Price: $55
Issued: 1999 • To Be Retired: 2000

2

Values
1E N/E
2E N/E
3E N/E
AE N/E

Wendy With Bronte, Keats, Tennyson And Poe…Wash Day
♪ *You Are So Beautiful*
#2771SF • Original Price: $45
Issued: 1998 • Retired: 1999

San Francisco Music Boxes

	Date Purchased	Price Paid	Value
1.			
2.			
	Totals		

The Doll Collection

In 1999, Boyds introduced a line of 12" open edition porcelain dolls so collectors would have more available alternatives to the 16" limited edition dolls. For Spring 2000, five additional 12" dolls and six more 16" dolls were released, bringing the total number of porcelain dolls to 42.

Values	
1E	$50
2E	$34
3E	$34
AE	$34

Allison With Andy ... Bird Watchin'
#4802 • Original Price: $34
Issued: 1999 • Current

New!

Values	
1E	$72
2E	$72
3E	$72
AE	$72

**Alyssa With Caroline & Carla ...
A Stitch In Time**
(LE-18,000, G.M.'s Choice)
#4928 • Original Price: $72
Issued: 2000 • To Be Retired: 2000

Values	
NE	$165

**Amy With Edwin ... Momma's
Clothes** (LE-18,000, G.M.'s Choice)
#4921 • Original Price: $100
Issued: 1999 • Retired: 1999

Porcelain Dolls

	Date Purchased	Price Paid	Value
1.			
2.			
3.			
4.			
Totals			

Values	
NE	$80

**Anne With Rockwell ...
The Masterpiece** (LE-12,000)
#4922 • Original Price: $72
Issued: 1999 • Retired: 1999

1

Value
NE $120

Betsy ... Sail Away (LE-12,000)
#4904 • Original Price: $69
Issued: 1998 • Retired: 1998

2

Values
1E $50
2E $38
3E $33.50
AE $33.50

Betsie With Troy ... A Day At The Lake
#4805 • Original Price: $33.50
Issued: 1999 • Current

3

Value
NE $100

Brittany ... Life's Journey
(LE-24,000, G.M.'s Choice)
#4906 • Original Price: $74
Issued: 1998 • Retired: 1998

4

Values
1E $80
2E $34
3E $34
AE $34

Brittany With Ben ... Goin' To Grandma's
#4803 • Original Price: $34
Issued: 1999 • Current

5

Value
NE $80

Candice With Macintosh ... Gathering Apples (LE-12,000)
#4923 • Original Price: $72
Issued: 1999 • Retired: 1999

Porcelain Dolls

	Date Purchased	Price Paid	Value
1.			
2.			
3.			
4.			
5.			

Totals

1

Values	
1E	$50
2E	$38
3E	$33.50
AE	$33.50

Catherine With Doolittle... The Nurse Is In
#4806 • Original Price: $33.50
Issued: 1999 • Current

2

Value	
NE	$80

Cheryl With Ashlie... Nighty Night (LE-12,000)
#4917 • Original Price: $69
Issued: 1999 • Retired: 1999

3

Value	
NE	$200

Elizabeth And Gary
(LE-25,000, QVC Exclusive, porcelain doll and figurine set,)
#4911V • Original Price: $116
Issued: 1998 • Retired: 1998

4 *New!*

Values	
1E	$37.50
2E	$37.50
3E	$37.50
AE	$37.50

Emilee With Otis... Forever
#4808 • Original Price: $37.50
Issued: 2000 • Current

Porcelain Dolls

	Date Purchased	Price Paid	Value
1.			
2.			
3.			
4.			
5.			

Totals

5

Value	
NE	$128

Emily ... The Future (LE-12,000)
#4902 • Original Price: $82
Issued: 1998 • Retired: 1998

Value Guide — Boyds Bears & Friends™

1
New!

Values	
1E	$34.50
2E	$34.50
3E	$34.50
AE	$34.50

Erica With Ferris . . . Carnival Fun
#4809 • Original Price: $34.50
Issued: 2000 • Current

2

Value	
NE	$80

Erin . . . Lemonade For Two
(LE-12,000)
#4915 • Original Price: $69
Issued: 1999 • Retired: 1999

3
New!

Values	
1E	$34.50
2E	$34.50
3E	$34.50
AE	$34.50

Erin Lynn With Squirt . . .
Peppermint Lemonade
#4810 • Original Price: $34.50
Issued: 2000 • Current

4

Value	
NE	$100

Jamie . . . The Last One (LE-12,000)
#4908 • Original Price: $69
Issued: 1998 • Retired: 1998

5

Value	
NE	$150

Jamie . . . The Last One
(LE-2,000, QVC Exclusive)
#4908-01V • Original Price: $66
Issued: 1998 • Retired: 1998

Porcelain Dolls

	Date Purchased	Price Paid	Value
1.			
2.			
3.			
4.			
5.			

Totals

195

1

Value
NE $92

Jean Marie With Nutmeg
(LE-3,000, QVC Exclusive)
#4919V • Original Price: N/A
Issued: 1999 • Retired: 1999

2

Value
NE $165

Jean With Nutmeg ... The Bakers
(LE-12,000)
#4919 • Original Price: $69
Issued: 1999 • Retired: 1999

3

New!

Values
1E $34.50
2E $34.50
3E $34.50
AE $34.50

Joni With Patch ... Strawberry Fields
#4812 • Original Price: $34.50
Issued: 2000 • Current

4

Value
NE $85

Julia ... Garden Friends
(LE-18,000, G.M.'s Choice)
#4912 • Original Price: $72
Issued: 1999 • Retired: 1999

Porcelain Dolls

	Date Purchased	Price Paid	Value
1.			
2.			
3.			
4.			
5.			

Totals

5

Value
NE $165

Karen ... Country Doll (LE-9,600)
#4900 • Original Price: $63
Issued: 1997 • Retired: 1997

1

Value
NE $80

Katherine ... Kind Hearts (LE-12,000)
#4910 • Original Price: $69
Issued: 1999 • Retired: 1999

2

Value
NE $80

Kayla With Kirby ... Harvest Time (LE-12,000)
#4918 • Original Price: $72
Issued: 1999 • Retired: 1999

3

Values
1E $50
2E $38
3E $33.50
AE $33.50

Kellie With Evan ... The Fun Of Collecting
#4804 • Original Price: $33.50
Issued: 1999 • Current

4

Value
NE $155

Kelly The Bear Collector (LE-12,000, QVC Exclusive)
#4916V • Original Price: $67
Issued: 1999 • Retired: 1999

5

Value
NE $115

Lara ... Moscow At Midnight (LE-12,000)
#4907 • Original Price: $71
Issued: 1998 • Retired: 1998

Porcelain Dolls

	Date Purchased	Price Paid	Value
1.			
2.			
3.			
4.			
5.			

Totals

Yesterday's Child...™ The Doll Collection

1

Value
NE $115

Laura ... First Day Of School
(LE-12,000)
#4903 • Original Price: $69
Issued: 1998 • Retired: 1998

2

Values
1E $80
2E $34
3E $34
AE $34

Laura With Lucy ... School Days
#4801 • Original Price: $34
Issued: 1999 • Current

3

New!

Values
1E $34.50
2E $34.50
3E $34.50
AE $34.50

Leah With Windy ... Summer Breeze
#4811 • Original Price: $34.50
Issued: 2000 • Current

4

New!

Value
NE $69

Lucinda With Gilligan ... By The Sea
(LE-12,000)
#4929 • Original Price: $69
Issued: 2000 • To Be Retired: 2000

Porcelain Dolls

	Date Purchased	Price Paid	Value
1.			
2.			
3.			
4.			
5.			

Totals

5

Value
NE $75

Melissa ... The Ballet (LE-12,000)
#4914 • Original Price: $69
Issued: 1999 • Retired: 1999

Value Guide — Boyds Bears & Friends™

1

New!

Value
NE $72

Molly With Cricket...
Winged Friends (LE-12,000)
#4924 • Original Price: $72
Issued: 2000 • To Be Retired: 2000

2

Value
NE $100

Ms. Ashley... The Teacher
(LE-12,000)
#4905 • Original Price: $69
Issued: 1998 • Retired: 1998

3

New!

Value
NE $72

Nicole With Buzz...
Sweeter Than Honey (LE-12,000)
#4925 • Original Price: $72
Issued: 2000 • To Be Retired: 2000

4

Values
1E $50
2E $38
3E $33.50
AE $33.50

Paige With Spinner...
Around The World
#4807 • Original Price: $33.50
Issued: 1999 • Current

5

New!

Value
NE $72

Rebecca With Elliot... Birthday
(LE-12,000)
#4927 • Original Price: $72
Issued: 2000 • To Be Retired: 2000

Porcelain Dolls

	Date Purchased	Price Paid	Value
1.			
2.			
3.			
4.			
5.			
		Totals	

Yesterday's Child... The Doll Collection

1 New!

Value
NE $72

Taylor With Jumper... Play Time
(LE-12,000)
#4926 • Original Price: $72
Issued: 2000 • To Be Retired: 2000

2

Value
NE $185

Victoria... City Doll (LE-9,600)
#4901 • Original Price: $63
Issued: 1997 • Retired: 1997

3

Value
NE $80

Wendy... Wash Day (LE-12,000)
#4909 • Original Price: $72
Issued: 1999 • Retired: 1999

Porcelain Dolls

	Date Purchased	Price Paid	Value
1.			
2.			
3.			

Totals

The Shoe Box Bears

Two more Grizbergs arrive for Spring 2000 along with "Paddy O'Beary ... Luck Of The Irish" who seems to have uncovered a pot of gold. These bears are clothed in creative costumes, unlike some of their other kin who arrived "bear nekkid."

Values	
PR	$62
1E	$52
2E	$35
3E	$30
AE	$28

Augustus "Gus" Grizberg
#3200 • Original Price: $19
Issued: 1996 • Retired: 1998

New!

Values	
1E	$11
2E	$11
3E	$11
AE	$11

Chicklet Grizberg ... A Sprinkle In Time
#3220 • Original Price: $11
Issued: 2000 • Current

Values	
1E	$36
2E	$24
3E	$17
AE	$17

Chief Sittingbear
#3218 • Original Price: $17
Issued: 1999 • Current

Values	
1E	$62
2E	$35
3E	$30
AE	$18

Elias "The Elf" Grizberg
#3206 • Original Price: $10
Issued: 1997 • Retired: 1999

General Figurines

	Date Purchased	Price Paid	Value
1.			
2.			
3.			
4.			
Totals			

Value Guide — Boyds Bears & Friends™

1

Values	
1E	$36
2E	$24
3E	$11
AE	$11

Ellie Grizberg ... Egg Hunter
#3212 • Original Price: $11
Issued: 1999 • To Be Retired: 2000

2

Values	
1E	$48
2E	$34
3E	$28
AE	$24

**Filbert Q. Foghorn ...
The Commodore**
#3208 • Original Price: $17
Issued: 1998 • Retired: 1999

3

Values	
PR	$64
1E	$52
2E	$38
3E	$32
AE	$28

Gertrude "Gertie" Grizberg
#3201 • Original Price: $15
Issued: 1996 • Retired: 1998

4

Value	
NE	$65

Gladys (NALED Exclusive)
#3201-01 • Original Price: $15
Issued: 1996 • Retired: 1996

General Figurines

	Date Purchased	Price Paid	Value
1.			
2.			
3.			
4.			
5.			

Totals

5

Values	
1E	$22
2E	$19
3E	$19
AE	$19

Ivan Mooselbeary
#3215 • Original Price: $19
Issued: 1999 • Current

Value Guide — Boyds Bears & Friends™

1

Values	
1E	$36
2E	$24
3E	$15
AE	$15

Ivy Mooselbeary
#3216 • Original Price: $15
Issued: 1999 • Current

2

Values	
1E	$52
2E	$37
3E	$30
AE	$22

Maisey "The Goil" Grizberg
#3203 • Original Price: $10
Issued: 1997 • Retired: 1998

3

Values	
1E	$50
2E	$34
3E	$28
AE	$24

Miles "Gobble" Grizberg
#3209 • Original Price: $17
Issued: 1998 • Retired: 1999

4

Values	
1E	$35
2E	$24
3E	$14
AE	$14

Momma Grizberg ... Egg Decorator
#3211 • Original Price: $14
Issued: 1999 • To Be Retired: 2000

5

Values	
1E	$52
2E	$38
3E	$30
AE	$26

Nicholas "Uncle Nick" Grizberg
#3205 • Original Price: $20
Issued: 1997 • Retired: 1999

General Figurines

	Date Purchased	Price Paid	Value
1.			
2.			
3.			
4.			
5.			

Totals

1

New!

Values	
1E	$14
2E	$14
3E	$14
AE	$14

Paddy O' Beary ...
Luck Of The Irish
#3221 • Original Price: $14
Issued: 2000 • Current

2

Values	
1E	$37
2E	$26
3E	$15
AE	$15

Princess Standingbear
#3217 • Original Price: $15
Issued: 1999 • Current

3

Values	
1E	$36
2E	$25
3E	$15
AE	$15

Sergeant Bookum O'Reilly ...
To Protect & Serve
#3214 • Original Price: $15
Issued: 1999 • Current

4

Values	
PR	$60
1E	$49
2E	$30
3E	$25
AE	$22

Thaddeus "Bud" Grizberg
#3202 • Original Price: $10
Issued: 1996 • Retired: 1998

General Figurines

	Date Purchased	Price Paid	Value
1.			
2.			
3.			
4.			
5.			

Totals

5

Value	
NE	$54

Uncle Irving Grizberg
(NALED Exclusive)
#3204-01 • Original Price: $20
Issued: 1997 • Retired: 1997

Value Guide — Boyds Bears & Friends™

1

Values	
1E	$50
2E	$35
3E	$28
AE	$22

Virginia "Ginny" Grizberg
#3210 • Original Price: $17
Issued: 1998 • Retired: 1999

2

New!

Values	
1E	$14
2E	$14
3E	$14
AE	$14

Webster Grizberg ... Just Duckie
#3219 • Original Price: $14
Issued: 2000 • Current

3

Values	
1E	$50
2E	$38
3E	$29
AE	$20

Winnie Hopkins & Bunnylove
#3207 • Original Price: $20
Issued: 1998 • To Be Retired: 2000

DeskAnimals

If you didn't capture one of these "wild" animals before December 31, 1999, you may have some hunting to do. The last of the current DeskAnimals were retired on that date, and no new critters have been spotted.

4

Value	
NE	$25

"Bob" Moosioswimius
#380001 • Original Price: $11
Issued: 1998 • Retired: 1999

General Figurines

	Date Purchased	Price Paid	Value
1.			
2.			
3.			

General Figurines

4.		

Totals

Value Guide — Boyds Bears & Friends™

1

Value
NE $13

"Lucy" Tigerocious Mommius
#380004 • Original Price: $11
Issued: 1998 • Retired: 1999

2

Value
NE $13

"Mel" Otterrificus
#380003 • Original Price: $11
Issued: 1998 • Retired: 1999

3

Value
NE $13

Puff Lochlegend
#380008 • Original Price: $11
Issued: 1999 • Retired: 1999

4

Value
NE N/E

Puff & Nessie Lochlegend
(QVC Exclusive, set/2)
#99647V • Original Price: $16
Issued: 1999 • Retired: 1999

General Figurines

	Date Purchased	Price Paid	Value
1.			
2.			
3.			
4.			
5.			

Totals

5

Value
NE $25

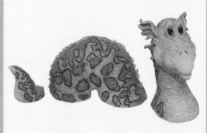

"Ray" Croccodiopius
#380000 • Original Price: $11
Issued: 1998 • Retired: 1999

1

Value
NE $13

Shelby Turtlecrawlius
#380007 • Original Price: $11
Issued: 1999 • Retired: 1999

2

Value
NE $13

"Smiley" Hippotoothocus
#380005 • Original Price: $11
Issued: 1998 • Retired: 1999

3

Value
NE $13

Spitz And Floyd Frogswimium …
Easy Method Swim School
#380006 • Original Price: $11
Issued: 1999 • Retired: 1999

4

Value
NE $25

"Zeb" Bearimonius Poppius
#380002 • Original Price: $11
Issued: 1998 • Retired: 1999

General Figurines

	Date Purchased	Price Paid	Value
1.			
2.			
3.			
4.			

Totals

Bearly-Built Villages

Six buildings and six groups of accessories mark the Spring 2000 debut of Boyds' new Bearly-Built Villages, home to Boyds Bears and Friends!

1

Values	
1E	$24
2E	$24
3E	$24
AE	$24

Bailey's Cozy Cottage
#19002
Original Price: $24
Issued: 2000 • Current

2

Values	
1E	$23
2E	$23
3E	$23
AE	$23

The Boyds Bearly A School
#19004
Original Price: $23
Issued: 2000 • Current

3

Values	
1E	$24
2E	$24
3E	$24
AE	$24

The Chapel In The Woods
#19003
Original Price: $24
Issued: 2000 • Current

4

Values	
1E	$25
2E	$25
3E	$25
AE	$25

Edmund's Hideaway
#19005
Original Price: $25
Issued: 2000 • Current

5

Values	
1E	$24
2E	$24
3E	$24
AE	$24

Public Libeary
#19006
Original Price: $24
Issued: 2000 • Current

6

Values	
1E	$24
2E	$24
3E	$24
AE	$24

Ted E. Bear Shop
#19001
Original Price: $24
Issued: 2000 • Current

Buildings

	Price Paid	Value
1.		
2.		
3.		
4.		
5.		
6.		

Accessories

7.		
8.		
9.		
10.		
11.		
12.		

Totals

7

Values	
1E	$8.50
2E	$8.50
3E	$8.50
AE	$8.50

Bailey's Cozy
Cottage Accessories
#19502-1
Original Price: $8.50
Issued: 2000 • Current

8

Values	
1E	$8.50
2E	$8.50
3E	$8.50
AE	$8.50

The Boyds Bearly A
School Accessories
#19504-1
Original Price: $8.50
Issued: 2000 • Current

9

Values	
1E	$8.50
2E	$8.50
3E	$8.50
AE	$8.50

The Chapel In The
Woods Accessories
#19503-1
Original Price: $8.50
Issued: 2000 • Current

10

Values	
1E	$8.50
2E	$8.50
3E	$8.50
AE	$8.50

Edmund's
Hideaway Accessories
#19505-1
Original Price: $8.50
Issued: 2000 • Current

11

Values	
1E	$8.50
2E	$8.50
3E	$8.50
AE	$8.50

Public Libeary Accessories
#19506-1
Original Price: $8.50
Issued: 2000 • Current

12

Values	
1E	$8.50
2E	$8.50
3E	$8.50
AE	$8.50

Ted E. Bear
Shop Accessories
#19501-1
Original Price: $8.50
Issued: 2000 • Current

Collector's Club

Members of The Loyal Order of Friends of Boyds (F.o.B.s, for short) are being treated to a "Tea for Three" themed collection in 2000. Members of the club receive tea party-themed membership pieces and may purchase several exclusive club pieces during the year.

1
1996

Value
NE $35

Raeburn
#01996-31 • Membership Gift
Issued: 1996 • Retired: 1997

2
1996

Value
NE $26

Uncle Elliot (pin)
#01996-11 • Membership Gift
Issued: 1996 • Retired: 1997

3
1996

Value
NE $95

Uncle Elliot...
The Head Bean Wants You
#01996-21 • Membership Gift
Issued: 1996 • Retired: 1997

4
1997

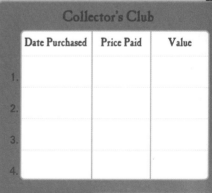

Value
NE $70

Velma Q. Berriweather
#01996-51 • Original Price: $29
Issued: 1997 • Retired: 1997

	Collector's Club		
	Date Purchased	Price Paid	Value
1.			
2.			
3.			
4.			
	Totals		

1 1997

Value
NE $80

Velma Q. Berriweather...
The Cookie Queen
#01996-41 • Original Price: $19
Issued: 1997 • Retired: 1997

2 1998

Value
NE N/E

Eleanor
#01998-31 • Membership Gift
Issued: 1998 • Retired: 1998

3 1998

Value
NE N/E

Lady Libearty (pin)
#01998-11 • Membership Gift
Issued: 1998 • Retired: 1998

4 1998

Value
NE $45

Lady Libearty
#01998-21 • Membership Gift
Issued: 1998 • Retired: 1998

Collector's Club

	Date Purchased	Price Paid	Value
1.			
2.			
3.			
4.			
5.			

Totals

5 1998

Value
NE $50

Ms. Berriweather's Cottage
#01998-41 • Original Price: $21
Issued: 1998 • Retired: 1998

Value Guide — Boyds Bears & Friends™

1
1998

Value
NE $60

Zelma G. Berriweather
#01998-51 • Original Price: $32
Issued: 1998 • Retired: 1998

2
1999

Value
NE N/E

Bloomin' F.o.B. (pin)
#01999-11 • Membership Gift
Issued: 1999 • Retired: 1999

3
1999

Value
NE $30

Blossum B. Berriweather...
Bloom With Joy!
#01999-21 • Membership Gift
Issued: 1999 • Retired: 1999

4
1999

Value
NE N/E

Flora Mae Berriweather
#01999-31 • Membership Gift
Issued: 1999 • Retired: 1999

5
1999

Value
NE $50

Noah's Genius At Work Table
Noah's Pageant Series
#2429 • Original Price: $11.50
Issued: 1999 • Retired: 1999

Collector's Club

	Date Purchased	Price Paid	Value
1.			
2.			
3.			
4.			
5.			

Totals

1

1999

Value
NE $46

Plant With Hope, Grow With Love, Bloom With Joy
#01999-51 • Original Price: $25
Issued: 1999 • Retired: 1999

2

1999

Value
NE $45

Sunny And Sally Berriweather ... Plant With Hope
#01999-41 • Original Price: $23
Issued: 1999 • Retired: 1999

3

New!

Value
NE N/E

Brewin' F.o.B. Mini-Tea Set
#02000-65 • Membership Gift
Issued: 2000 • To Be Retired: 2000

4

New!

Value
NE N/E

Caitlin Berriweather (pin)
#02000-11 • Membership Gift
Issued: 2000 • To Be Retired: 2000

Collector's Club

	Date Purchased	Price Paid	Value
1.			
2.			
3.			
4.			
5.			

Totals

5

New!

Value
NE N/E

Caitlin Berriweather
#02000-31 • Membership Gift
Issued: 2000 • To Be Retired: 2000

Value Guide — Boyds Bears & Friends™

1 New!

Value
NE N/E

Catherine And Caitlin Berriweather ...Fine Cup Of Tea
#02000-21 • Membership Gift
Issued: 2000 • To Be Retired: 2000

2 New!

Value
NE N/E

Catherine And Caitlin Berriweather With Little Scruff ... Family Traditions
#02000-41 • Original Price: $25
Issued: 2000 • To Be Retired: 2000

3 New!

Value
NE N/E

Catherine Berriweather And Little Scruff
#02000-51 • Original Price: $26
Issued: 2000 • To Be Retired: 2000

4 New!

Value
NE N/E

Noah's Tool Box
#2434 • Original Price: $12
Issued: 2000 • To Be Retired: 2000

Collector's Club

	Date Purchased	Price Paid	Value
1.			
2.			
3.			
4.			

Totals

Future Releases

Use this page to record future BOYDS releases.

The Bearstone Collection	Orig. Price	Status	Market Value						Price Paid	Value
			PR	1E	2E	3E	AE	NE		
The Folkstone Collection										
The Purrstone Collection										

Page Total:	Price Paid	Total Value

Future Releases

Use this page to record future BOYDS releases.

Yesterday's Child The Dollstone Collection	Orig. Price	Status	Market Value						Price Paid	Value
			PR	1E	2E	3E	AE	NE		
Yesterday's Child . . . The Doll Collection										
The Shoe Box Bears										
DeskAnimals										
Bearly-Built Villages										
The Loyal Order of Friends of Boyds										

Page Total:	Price Paid	Total Value

Total Value Of My Collection

Record the value of your collection here!

The Bearstone Collection			The Bearstone Collection		
Page Number	Price Paid	Market Value	Page Number	Price Paid	Market Value
Page 37			Page 71		
Page 38			Page 72		
Page 39			Page 73		
Page 40			Page 74		
Page 41			Page 75		
Page 42			Page 76		
Page 43			Page 77		
Page 44			Page 78		
Page 45			Page 79		
Page 46			Page 80		
Page 47			Page 81		
Page 48			Page 82		
Page 49			Page 83		
Page 50			Page 84		
Page 51			Page 85		
Page 52			Page 86		
Page 53			Page 87		
Page 54			Page 88		
Page 55			Page 89		
Page 56			Page 90		
Page 57			Page 91		
Page 58			Page 92		
Page 59			Page 93		
Page 60			Page 94		
Page 61			Page 95		
Page 62			Page 96		
Page 63			Page 97		
Page 64			Page 98		
Page 65			Page 99		
Page 66			Page 100		
Page 67			Page 101		
Page 68			Page 102		
Page 69			Page 103		
Page 70			Page 104		
Subtotal			Subtotal		

	Price Paid	Value
Page Total:		

Transfer the totals from each Value Guide page onto these Total Value Of My Collection worksheets, then add the page totals together to determine the overall value (the Grand Total) of your collection.

The Folkstone Collection			The Folkstone Collection		
Page Number	Price Paid	Market Value	Page Number	Price Paid	Market Value
Page 105			Page 137		
Page 106			Page 138		
Page 107			Page 139		
Page 108			Page 140		
Page 109			Page 141		
Page 110			Page 142		
Page 111			Page 143		
Page 112			Page 144		
Page 113			Page 145		
Page 114			Page 146		
Page 115			Page 147		
Page 116			Page 148		
Page 117			Page 149		
Page 118			Page 150		
Page 119			Page 151		
Page 120			Page 152		
Page 121			Page 153		
Page 122			Page 154		
Page 123			Page 155		
Page 124			Page 156		
Page 125			Page 157		
Page 126			Page 158		
Page 127			Page 159		
Page 128			Page 160		
Page 129			Page 161		
Page 130			Page 162		
Page 131			Page 163		
Page 132			Page 164		
Page 133			Page 165		
Page 134			Page 166		
Page 135			Page 167		
Page 136			Page 168		
Subtotal			Subtotal		

	Price Paid	Value
Page Total:		

The Purrstone Collection

Page Number	Price Paid	Market Value
Page 169		
Page 170		
Page 171		
Subtotal		

Yesterdays Child • The Dollstone Collection

Page Number	Price Paid	Market Value
Page 172		
Page 173		
Page 174		
Page 175		
Page 176		
Page 177		
Page 178		
Page 179		
Page 180		
Page 181		
Page 182		
Page 183		
Page 184		
Page 185		
Page 186		
Page 187		
Page 188		
Page 189		
Page 190		
Page 191		
Subtotal		

Yesterdays Child . . . The Doll Collection

Page Number	Price Paid	Market Value
Page 192		
Page 193		
Page 194		
Page 195		
Page 196		
Page 197		
Page 198		
Page 199		
Page 200		
Subtotal		

The Shoe Box Bears/DeskAnimals

Page Number	Price Paid	Market Value
Page 201		
Page 202		
Page 203		
Page 204		
Page 205		
Page 206		
Page 207		
Subtotal		

Bearly-Built Villages

Page Number	Price Paid	Market Value
Page 208		
Subtotal		

The Loyal Order of Friends of Boyds

Page Number	Price Paid	Market Value
Page 209		
Page 210		
Page 211		
Page 212		
Page 213		
Subtotal		

Page Total:	Price Paid	Value

Add the "Page Totals" together
to find your "Grand Total."

GRAND TOTAL	Price Paid	Total Value

Variations

*T*he charming creations of Gary Lowenthal have person-alities all their own. This means that one piece may be slightly different from the others. So if you have a piece that doesn't look quite the same as its picture in the Collector's Value Guide™, don't fret! It just may be one of the many variations found within the world of The Boyds Collection Ltd.

Lowenthal's creativity knows no bounds when he sets out to design each new piece. But once a piece has been produced, "The Head Bean" might decide that a bear looks too furry or an angel's arm isn't long enough, and the company will correct those "flaws."

Sometimes, even after a piece has been released, Lowenthal may decide to overhaul the piece completely and create an entirely new mold, one that shows definite changes. But Boyds variations aren't limited to obvious details. Some pieces might have slight color differences, such as a new shade of blue for a bear's sweater. And in some cases, Boyds may even give a piece an entirely new name after several editions have been released.

To find out if a collectible is a variation or a different item, compare it with a genuine piece at a retail shop and look at variations listed in a reputable guide, such as the Collector's Value Guide™. See if the names and item numbers on the bottoms are the same. Following are examples of some of the more common types of variations.

Sometimes It's Obvious . . .

STANDARD VERSION

VARIATION

BAILEY BEAR WITH SUIT-CASE (#2000) – Between trips, Bailey must have gotten her fur trimmed! In most editions of this piece, Bailey's texture is rough and detailed. But there's another version with a smooth and more colorful surface. It may look as though it's a different piece, but the names and style numbers on the bottoms are the same.

STANDARD VERSION

VARIATION

BAILEY THE BAKER . . . WITH SWEETIE PIE (#2254) – In this variation, Bailey takes time to show her love for Clarion, Iowa. During the town's June 1995 Teddy Bear Festival, 3,600 of these figurines were produced with the words "CLARION . . . IOWA" carved onto the pie that she is holding. This "Clarion Bear," as it is known, also wears a different color dress and head ribbon.

FATHER CHRISBEAR AND SON (#2008) – The original version of this piece showed this bear and cub without a base to sit upon. But they must have complained of the cold, because Boyds later provided them with a base upon which to sit.

Then There Are The Details . . .

BAILEY . . . THE GRADUATE – CARPE DIEM (#227701-10) – In some versions of this piece, you can see how excited Bailey is about her impending graduation because her eyes are huge! In later editions, her eyes are a much smaller size.

STANDARD VERSION

VARIATION

BYRON & CHEDDA WITH CATMINT (#2010) – This little guy can't seem to make up his mind what he wants to wear! Some editions of this piece show him with stitching on his hat, or a patch sewn on his arm.

STANDARD VERSION

VARIATION

MINERVA . . . THE BASEBALL ANGEL (#2826) – This sports fan must have changed clothes during the seventh inning stretch. She first appeared wearing a dress with six buttons below her belt, but later changed into a dress that has seven buttons.

GRENVILLE & BEATRICE . . .
BEST FRIENDS (#2016) – Doves
sure do get around! In one version of this figurine, a dove
appears on the front center of
the base, while on another
version, the dove is positioned
on the base's right side.

STANDARD VERSION

VARIATION

What's In A Name?

LUCKY MCPLUG (#2871) – This guy wasn't always "Lucky." His
original name was "Sparky McPlug."

PEACENIK . . . THE SIXTIES SANTA (#2809) – When this piece
was first released, this Santa Claus was known as "Peace-Nick."

ZIP SHOVELENHAND . . . GOT SNOW? (#28104) – Originally,
this fella' was called "Zambonie . . . Got Snow?"

And Bear In Mind . . .

Two completely different pieces may be mistaken as variations.
Pieces such as "Grenville With Green Scarf" (#2003-04) and
"Grenville With Red Scarf" (#2003-08) may look similar, but they
are actually two separate pieces.

Boyds also makes Canadian exclusives that may look similar to
its American versions. For example, "Chelsea Kainada . . . The
Practice" (#BC22851) resembles "Margot . . . The Ballerina"
(#227709) with slightly different colors; however, these pieces are not
the same.

To confuse collectors further, even the same name doesn't always
mean the same piece! The Canadian version of "Lefty On The
Mound" (#BC2066) is almost identical to its American counterpart
(#2253). But don't be fooled by the same name and slightly different
colors. They are entirely separate pieces with totally different item
numbers and secondary market values.

The Secondary Market

Collecting Boyds figurines can become habit-forming. Before you know it, you may find yourself wanting every piece ever made! Unfortunately, that might be hard to do. As with other collectibles, Boyds retires a number of pieces each year, making them hard to find.

Fortunately, Boyds informs its fans of upcoming retirements so collectors can plan accordingly. But it's still easy to miss out on owning a piece that was retired long ago, especially if it was a limited edition. This is why savvy collectors turn to the secondary market.

How To Get Started . . .

One traditional secondary market option is an exchange service that deals in retired and hard-to-find collectibles. Most exchanges provide listings of the pieces that collectors wish to purchase or sell, as well as an asking price. Exchanges may publish these lists on a monthly or a daily basis, and typically distribute this information to collectors who purchase a subscription or pay a membership fee.

Bears In Cyberspace . . .

With the advent of the Internet, there's a whole new way to find and purchase Boyds pieces on-line. You can also communicate with collectors around the world, and possibly uncover information about your favorite Boyds pieces.

If you type "Boyds Bears" into your computer's search engine, you'll find links to on-line stores and web pages of other collectors. Sometimes a collector may be selling a portion of his or her collection, and will show a picture of each piece for sale. If there's no picture, be cautious about the piece's authenticity or quality. If you're looking for something a little more specific, try a message board, a chat room for Boyds collectors or an on-line auction. Many of these sites have links for collectible items, or even a special site for Boyds in particular. Best of all, there just might be someone on-line who has the piece you want – and you'll meet other folks who share your passion for collecting Boyds.

Buyer Beware . . .

Before you jump into any deal that seems too good to be true, there are some things to consider. Certain factors affect the value and price of any Boyds piece. Know how to recognize these factors before you take out your checkbook.

In order to keep track of how many pieces are produced, Boyds numbers many of its pieces. On the bottom of each piece, you'll find an edition number (such as "1E," which means "First Edition"). Following that mark is the piece's number within that edition.

Each Bearstone figurine has 6,000 pieces in each edition, except for the *Holiday Pageant* and *Noah's Pageant* series, which have 7,200 apiece. Each Folkstone figurine currently has 6,000 pieces, as do the Dollstones, Purrstones and The Shoe Box Bears. The Bearly-Built Villages pieces have edition sizes of 5,100 pieces. In general, the most valuable and desired pieces in any series are the first, or earliest, editions, so before any purchase, find out which edition is for sale.

Resin figurines sometimes do get damaged. A chip or crack may reduce the secondary market value, so before you but a piece, be sure to check to see if there's any damage. And remember, a collectible is considered to be in "mint condition" only if it comes with its original box.

There's no doubt about it. Collecting truly is a fun pastime, but the real thrill is often in the hunt. There are few things more satisfying than tacking down all those "must-have" pieces to help make your collection complete!

Dealers, Exchanges & Newsletters

BOYDS BEAR RETAIL INQUIRER
P.O. Box 4385
Gettysburg, PA 17325
(general Boyds newsletter written by "The Head Bean Hisself")

BEAR TALES & TRAILS
Millie & Harry Croft
518 N. Everett Drive
Palatine, IL 60067-4110
(847) 358-6276
beartales@pipeline.com

COLLECTIBLE EXCHANGE, INC.
6621 Columbiana Road
New Middletown, OH 44442
(216) 542-9646

DONNA'S COLLECTIBLES EXCHANGE
703 Endeavor Drive South
Winter Springs, FL 32708
1-800-480-5105
www.donnascollexch.com

THE FORBEARS COLLECTIBLES
David & Sandi Goerzen
297 E. Mill Avenue
Porterville, CA 93257-3935
(559) 781-1205
theforbears@ocsnet.net

ED & JANET HYMES
Edlen Estates
Lot 104
Jacksonville, IL 62650
(217) 245-4603
(secondary market dealer only)

LIONS, TIGERS, AND BOYDS, OH, MY!!!
Laurie Anne Greez
P.O. Box 1393
Easton, MA 02334-1393
(newsletter only)

NEW ENGLAND COLLECTIBLES EXCHANGE
Bob Dorman
201 Pine Avenue
Clarksburg, MA 01247
(413) 663-3643
nece@collectiblesbroker.com
www.collectiblesbroker.com

OPINIONS
Joanne Libke
117 Twin Brooks Cove
Edmonton, Alberta, Canada
T6J-6T1
(780) 436-3120
josclans@connect.ab.ca
(Boyds pin guide)

Production & Packaging

*E*very Boyds creation begins in one of the zaniest places on Earth – inside Gary Lowenthal's own mind! First, he brings each piece to life on paper with a sketch. After that, artists make a three-dimensional version out of clay. After it has been revised and altered to meet Boyds' high standards of excellence, the new piece will be approved as a "white ware" original mold.

As soon as Lowenthal and his artists choose the right colors for the piece, it's time to start casting. Each piece receives an item number, as well as an appropriate quote. So far, Boyds has used quotations from such famous people as William Shakespeare and Jack Benny. And each edition number is hand written, giving each piece a personal touch.

But a Boyds figurine would be incomplete without a name. Lowenthal has named some of his figurines after his wife and children – even himself. And he has discovered some unusual and old-fashioned names by randomly asking people on the street the names of their relatives.

A Box For Every Line

Each collection has its own unique box. Bearstones are shipped to retailers in dark green boxes with maroon trim, while Folkstones come in maroon boxes trimmed in dark green. *The Wee Folkstones* are packaged in their own boxes that resemble vine-covered stone walls.

In keeping with their rustic look, *Carvers Choice* pieces come in plain cardboard boxes. The Dollstones boxes, however, are yellow with maroon designs. The new Purrstone creations come in dark blue boxes with yellow trim. And, finally, the Shoe Box Bears come in a replica of – what else? – a shoe box!

Insuring Your Collection

Insuring your Boyds collection is a good idea, since a large collection can be worth thousands of dollars. But there are some points collectors should be aware of before obtaining insurance.

Know exactly what is in your collection and how much it's worth. Keep records of how you built your collection – save all your receipts and be sure to document each item, noting the date it was bought, how much you paid and if the item has a special status, such as being a limited edition or retired. Keeping your receipts and purchase information in a safe-deposit box is recommended. Since the values of Boyds' pieces increase with time, you also need to keep track of each item's value so it can be insured for the correct amount.

Learn as much as possible about your coverage. Collectibles are often included in homeowner's or renter's insurance, although some policies don't cover certain accidents. Find out what your policy does cover, and also what documentation you will need if something happens to your pieces. Most insurance companies will not compensate a loss without proof of its value. Many companies will accept a reputable secondary market price guide – such as the Collector's Value Guide™ – as a valid source for determining your collection's value. You'll also need to notify your insurance carrier about changes in the value of your collection.

Assess how much coverage you need. Some companies offer specific policies for collectible items, or can add a "rider," or additional coverage, to your homeowner's insurance policy. When you know how much your collection is worth, you can then decide how to best insure it. When making this decision, weigh the cost of replacing your collection against the cost of insuring it.

Bearfinder — Numerical Index

Pieces are listed in numerical order by item number, followed by page number and picture box.

Bearfinder — Alphabetical Index

Pieces are listed in alphabetical order by item number, follwed by page number and picture box.

Look

COLLECTOR'S
VALUE GUIDE™

for our best-selling titles:

Boyds Bears & Friends™
Boyds Plush Animals
Charming Tails®
Cherished Teddies®
Department 56® **Snowbabies**™
Department 56® **Villages**
Dreamsicles®
Fifty State Quarters™
Hallmark Keepsake Ornamer
Harbour Lights®
Harmony Kingdom®
Pokémon™
PRECIOUS MOMENTS®
Ty® **Beanie Babies**®
Ty® **Plush Animals**

Find these at fine gift and collectibles stores
everywhere. For more information call toll-free: **877-722-020**

Discover

a World of Collectibles Information

CollectorBee.com

- *Read daily news features!*
- *Discover our interactive bulletin board!*
- *Find great links to all your favorite collecti*
- *Subscribe to the our free e-mail newsletter!*

Don't Wait! Get In Touch
With The Wonderful World
Of Collectibles Today!

CheckerBee
PUBLISHIN

306 Industrial Park Road | Middletown, CT 0645
800 746 3686 | www.CollectorBee.co

Boyds Bears & Friends™
presents the

≋ The Loyal Order of ≋
Friends of Boyds
Year 2000 Collectors' Club

A Slightly Off-Center Collector's Club
for people who still believe in...

Bears and Hares You Can Trust™

R.S.V.P. to become a
"Brewin' F.o.B!"

And have we got a story for you, turn the page ☞

Here's how to join.

PLEASE PRINT

CHECK ONE: ❏ Current/Former Member ID# _____
❏ New Member

NAME _____

ADDRESS _____

CITY _____

STATE _____ ZIP CODE _____

DAYTIME PHONE (_____) _____

E-MAIL ADDRESS _____

DATE OF BIRTH *(year optional)* _____

❏ I want to be a "Brewin' F.o.B." for
    the Year 2000 for a measly . . .   **$32.50**
  (NY & Texas Residents add 8 1/4% sales tax = $35.18)

❏ I want to join for Two Years for just $63.00 _____
  (NY & Texas Residents add 8 1/4% sales tax = $68.20)
❏ And throw in the "Brewin' F.o.B."
  Official Mini-Tea Set, too, for   **$7.50**
  (NY & Texas Residents add 8 1/4% sales tax = $8.12)
    My Grand Total is _____

FORM OF PAYMENT:

❏ Check ❏ Money Order ❏ Master Card ❏ Visa

CREDIT CARD NUMBER: (Exp. Date __/__)

MAKE PAYABLE TO: The Boyds Collection Ltd.®
P.O. Box 4386 F.o.B. Dept.
Gettysburg, PA 17325-4386

Authorized Signature:

_____

*(Authorized signature must accompany charge request.
Card will be processed at time of shipment.)*

I understand that my membership kit will be shipped 12 to 16 weeks
following receipt of this application at The Boyds Collection Ltd.
Offer Expires December 31, 2000

WHO IS YOUR RETAILER?

(you know the place where you purchase your Boyds stuff)

Name _____ ID# _____

City _____ State _____ Zip _____

Join us, won't you?

But first...let us set the proper Mood for the year 2000 Club Kit. Take a deep breath, relax and imagine...a Quiet Corner with sunbeams dancing through the windowpanes...a table set for Three. Sugar cubes and those tiny tongs...a Teapot with the aroma of lightly scented steam rising. Delicate china Cups and Saucers handed down from Great-Grandmother who carefully packed them for her long journey across the sea many years ago. A child-sized chair or two, and a visit from a raggedy, but dearly loved friend...these are the ingredients in "Tea for Three" our Brewin' F.o.B. story for the Year 2000.

Exclusive Pieces

Join **Caitlin Berriweather**, the member-exclusive 6" gold Plush Bear who is always ready to listen to a Great Story...or share a few Tales of her own! Caitlin is always properly Dressed for the Occasion in her Hat and Chenille Sweater...and has a special foot pad F.o.B. label.

The Brewin' F.o.B. Kit will also include our 3-1/4" Bearstone™ Masterpiece "**Catherine and Caitlin Berriweather...Fine Cup of Tea**". You can almost hear the tea pourin' amongst the Chatter (and Boyds bears aren't known for daintily doing anything!)

Club members will also receive The "Brewin' F.o.B." Bearwear Pin, 2-1/4", portraying Caitlin Berriweather enjoying her beverage of choice. Club pins are a great way to proudly show off your love of Boyds...unless you would rather keep it a Secret. (Can't blame you there!)

Your Club Kit will also include a heart-warming poem, "**Tea for Three**" that perfectly captures the Mood. The poem is 5" x 7" and Suitable for Framin'...just in case you want to hang it near the door as a little Reminder of the important things in life...or set it up next to your Plush and Resin pieces!

Other great stuff will include:

🐾 The updated Boyds Bears & Friends pocket-sized **Product List** - so you know what to look for when you're on the Hunt for Boyds.

🐾 The **Boyds Dealer Directory** for 2000 - so you know where to hunt for the "Bears and Hares...You Can Trust."

🐾 A year's subscription (four big issues) of the **F.o.B. Bear Inquirer**...all the Boyds News that's fit to print...and then some. Find out if the Head Bean really does sleep with his bear ears on! (Just kiddin'...some information is just too personal, and do you <u>really</u> want to know?!)

PLUS...for the first time in Boyds History...your Membership Number entitles you to enter the "VIP" part of our new Website, www.BoydsCollectibles.com, where only "Brewin' F.o.Bs" can go! You'll find even more Insider News, Hot Stories, the complete Scoop on our terrific products...and much more.

And the Head Bean has done it again!
NO price increase for The Loyal Order of Friends of Boyds members — $32.50 is still the price for all this great stuff. So pinkies up...and start sippin'.

There's more! No Tea Party would be complete without a Tea Set...or a Mini Tea-Set in this case. Members Only will have the opportunity to purchase the Official Brewin' F.o.B. Mini-Tea Set...for three of course! Just mark your Application to receive your Tea Set with your kit.

2-3/4" H

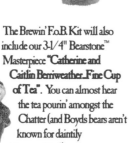

There's a place set just for you at our Tea Party.